HOW TO SELECT, TRAIN, AND BREED YOUR DOG

HOW TO SELECT, TRAIN, AND BREED YOUR DOG

by LEON F. WHITNEY, D.V.M.

DAVID McKAY COMPANY, INC.
New York

HOW TO SELECT, TRAIN, AND BREED YOUR DOG

LIBRARY OF CONGRESS CATALOG CARD NUMBER: 68-31284
MANUFACTURED IN THE UNITED STATES OF AMERICA
VAN REES PRESS • NEW YORK

To Julie

Contents

vii

Author's Note

As a veterinarian having raised so many thousand dogs and having studied them, everything from heredity to the effect of de-worming drugs, it has long seemed to me a duty to put this material in a book that would be helpful to the widest possible number of people interested in dogs.

My book about puppies for the one-dog owner, written in 1955, has had an excellent sale, but it covers only a small segment of the whole field. There are hundreds of dog lovers who have no idea which breeds would be best for their families. There are thousands of whelpings every year from bitches whose owners have no idea what to do nor how to manage them. That these people are eager for the information, I know, from my constant consultations and frequent—sometimes desperate—telephone calls.

In addition there are those owners who would like to know *why* they do this or that. For such folks and particularly for the inquiring youngsters, I believe answers to all pertinent questions should be available. In this book, therefore, I've tried to pack every item of useful information about dogs from the time a bitch is ready to be bred until the puppies are mature.

HOW TO SELECT, TRAIN, AND
BREED YOUR DOG

Chapter One

WHAT PUPPY IS RIGHT FOR YOU?

Buying a dog is a momentous step. You are choosing a pet that should be a source of enjoyment, protection, companionship, and pride for some dozen years. Therefore it is important to select just the right one for your family.

SELECTING THE PUPPY

The dog's size

Your choice of dog should be governed by many considerations. Where you live—city, country, or suburbs—is important, and so is how you live and who you are. Because there is such a wide variety in human and canine temperaments, it pays to choose the dog that suits your likes and dislikes. You won't be as well satisfied with a large outdoor dog in a small house or apartment as with a small or medium-sized one. I'm not suggesting that big dogs can't be happy in apartments, but they do require a great deal of space. On a farm you need a larger dog. But again the question of your likes and wants enters.

His usefulness

Do you need a watchdog? Then buy one of the watchdog breeds—a German shepherd, a Doberman pinscher, or a bull terrier. Do you want a dog that will be a companion for your children? Then one with a herding instinct is excellent—a farm shepherd or a collie. A gentle cocker spaniel and many others that are not herders are admirably suited for children too. Perhaps you prefer a dog that will be both pet for the family and hunter for your husband and son. Bird dogs and most of the hounds make excellent pets as well as superlative hunters. Duck hunters need retrievers. Upland game hunters prefer setters and pointers (the former usually make better pets). Beagles are affectionate pets as well as good rabbit dogs. Coon hunters want coon hounds, which usually become family pets too.

Your location

The section of the country in which you live must influence your choice to a considerable degree. Outdoor dogs in the North should have thick, heavy coats; in the deep South they should be short-haired, or, if long-haired, they should be thin-coated. You may also have to consider such matters as whether there is a brook or pond near your home. Some dogs love water and they'll become a nuisance by constantly plunging into the water and rolling in the mud.

Incidentally, your choice of a breed shouldn't be based on the fact that another of the breed is a motion-picture hero. Remember that the movie dog has had expert training. You might find that your dog won't be as affectionate, loyal, and courageous.

And don't for a minute think that you can learn anything but good things about the various breeds by reading breed books. For one thing the authors are usually show people whose interest is in principally breeding for looks almost regardless of temperament or native ability. For another thing the books are written to sell the breeds they describe. Suppose you owned a pet store. Along comes an honest and unprejudiced book about Alsatians (German shepherds). Lots of Alsatian breeders come to the store. Most of them never owned a dog of any other breed. They buy the book because they love to read all the good things about "their breed." They find an honest but derogatory sentence. Their fur flies. They rush back to the seller and tell him, "Unless you quit selling these terrible books I shall never patronize your store again."

That's not all. Another book buyer buys a copy, and he reads the truth too. The pet shop owner does a big business in Alsatians. The book lost him a sale. Out it goes.

Even *Pure Bred Dogs,* officially published by the American Kennel Club, has nothing but complimentary words about every breed!

VARIETIES OF BREEDS

When you have decided on the general *type* of dog you want, compare the characteristics of the various breeds in that category. The chart in the next chapter and my thumbnail description of some of the important breeds will, I think, help you to make your choice. Also, study pictures of the champions of the breed you plan to purchase. Whether you choose a dog mainly for usefulness or for its attractive appearance, don't overlook personality and temperament.

Then there is the matter of the strain within the breed. Learn all you can about the particular characteristics of that strain from those who know it. In time every dog breeder tends to develop a strain with some outstanding features. This is due to the fact that one stud dog has been used principally in creating that strain. The best people to consult in the matter of strain characteristics are veterinarians, dog judges, and professional handlers of show dogs. They are usually free from bias, because they are not trying to induce you to buy a specific breed or strain of dog.

Some strains within breeds are not typical of the breed. Thus it is wise to see the parents of any dog or puppy you are considering. Handle them; see if you can make one growl. Look for any undesirable traits which might have been transmitted to their offspring.

Unless you are buying the dog chiefly for show purposes, don't be overimpressed with show records or pedigrees. A dog with an unpleasant disposition is an inferior specimen of his breed no matter how long and star-studded his pedigree.

MALE OR FEMALE?

This is undoubtedly a question you'll ask. A whole book could be written on this subject, but here, in brief, are the points to be considered:

Males tend to be more aggressive, grow slightly larger and become stronger, are better protectors, and can be used for stud, provided they are superlative specimens and have demonstrated that fact by winning at field trials or at shows.

As pets, males have the following disadvantages: they are inclined to become restless and uneasy when bitches in the neighborhood are in season or when your own are in season, they wet on your evergreen shrubbery or on that of your neighbors, and are more pugnacious, especially if they are of a naturally pugnacious breed.

Females tend to be more affectionate and non-aggressive, can be used to perpetuate the breed or may be spayed if no puppies are desired, squat down to urinate and do not harm shrubbery.

Disadvantages of females are the necessity of confining or boarding them twice a year, and perhaps even then having all the neighborhood male dogs camping at your home, the not infrequent complications of diseases of the reproductive tract, and having to raise unwanted litters of puppies if the bitch is accidentally bred.

If the dog you choose is a male, look or feel to be sure both of his testicles are in the scrotum before you buy him. Unlike human beings, the testicles have descended to where they belong by the time the pup is born. If they are not in the proper place, don't buy him unless you plan to have the pup castrated anyway. True, injections of the right hormone will often cause them to descend, or a veterinary surgeon can remove the retained one or both, but why burden yourself with such a problem?

GROOMING

Also consider carefully the matter of grooming, remembering that while all dogs shed, long-haired ones are obviously more generous in this respect. Moreover, long-haired dogs have to be combed. If the hair is straight and rather coarse, occasional combing will keep the coat in excellent condition; but silky hair, which mats easily, needs much more attention.

If your pet requires professional grooming, the cost of his upkeep rises substantially. Having a wire-haired terrier plucked or clipped two or three times a year costs from six dollars to twenty dollars. Some spaniels need three or four clippings a year; the cost is between six dollars and fifteen dollars. Keeping a French poodle trimmed costs at least ten dollars annually (some owners spend as much as two hundred dollars).

FEEDING COST

In making your choice, consider, too, the question of food. A large dog fed on table scraps consumes at least as much as one person, or, if fed sensibly on dry dog food, he may be fed for fifteen cents a day. Ask yourself, Am I going to be willing to make my dog eat what I know is good for him, or am I the kind of person who can't resist those pleading eyes when a dog begs for tasty human food? It is so easy to spoil a dog!

PUREBRED OR MONGREL?

Perhaps you wonder whether only a purebred dog makes a really satisfactory pet. Not at all; some mongrels are delightful pets. The chief difference between the two is that a purebred's temperament is more predictable. He has a long history of breeding, with a recognized standard of performance and appearance. However, disappointments sometimes occur even when you have investigated the dog or puppy as thoroughly as possible.

Some people have the mistaken notion that a dog whose parents are purebreds of different breeds—for example, a purebred Dalmatian and a purebred cocker spaniel—is not a mongrel. Any dog produced by crossing two breeds is a mongrel. His chief drawback is his unpredictability. However, if a puppy's father and mother have been mated several times before, you can learn a great deal about your puppy's mental and physical attributes by observing the characteristics of his older brothers and sisters.

Chapter Two

HOW AND WHERE TO BUY YOUR DOG

It is now important that we look into the chief ways of obtaining dogs. Where, from whom, and in what manner should you buy your pet?

THE BREEDER

If you can visit the kennel of a breeder and personally select a puppy, you have a better chance of obtaining what you want than when buying in any other way. You may be able to see the father and mother, handle them, observe any abnormalities or weaknesses, see if they are shy, and if their bladder sphincter muscles are normal or if they piddle when petted. You can also make sure that their vision and hearing are acute.

Then, there may be brothers and sisters from other litters in the kennel that will give you a good idea what kind of producers the parents are.

You can inquire about vaccinations, dewormings, feeding and training, particularly with regard to housebreaking.

There may be a whole litter to choose from. If you want a large example of the breed, select the largest pup, because early size is at least a partial indication that the pup will eventually be big—although this is by no means certain. Select the pup that most appeals to you on all points. Some people take the one which seems to cozy up to them the most, but I advise against letting the pup choose you.

Yes, personal selection at the kennel, once you have decided on the breed, is the most satisfactory way of choosing a puppy.

THE PET SHOP

The pet-shop owner is a middleman between the breeder and buyer. He either buys puppies or takes them on consignment, and sells them to his customers. Usually a number of the "cutest" of these puppies are placed in the shop windows as "attention-getters." You may be among those watching the puppies frolic, and if you are a person who finds it hard to resist such cuteness and decides then and there to buy, here are some points to consider:

(1) The puppy stays cute for a very short time.

(2) You cannot see the puppy's parents, so you have no way of being reasonably sure how it will grow up.

(3) The pet-shop owner's integrity is your best basis for knowing about the pup. He can tell you how others from the same breeding have developed and how reliable the breeder is.

(4) If you want a purebred dog, be certain the puppy is typical of puppies of that breed.

(5) Inquire about what disease protection the pup has had. Was serum administered? When? Was it permanently immunized? How? These are questions your veterinarian will ask should you later take your puppy for treatment.

(6) Inquire about what treatments have been given for intestinal parasites. You'll know when to deworm the

pup again or when the veterinarian should do it for you.

(7) Put most of your money into the dog and not into a lot of "equipment."

Some pet-shop owners know a great many breeders and have had experience with their reliability. Often they can even help you in buying a dog of a breed they do not have for sale. It may pay you well to consult a reliable dealer.

Still another, and related, source is the professional handler. These people exhibit dogs for fees and often know where the best puppies are to be had. If there is a professional handler in your locality, you may be wise to consult him, for among his clients may be a breeder of the very dog you want.

MAIL ORDER

Buying a puppy which you see and buying one by mail are quite different propositions. One can be terribly disappointed in mail-bought dogs. I should know. Not only have I had disappointments of my own, but you can well imagine the hundreds of sad stories I've listened to from those who brought their dogs for veterinary attention or for health certificates needed when returning dogs to the seller. Most states require health certificates on all dogs or puppies coming from other states. This means that should you buy a dog that proves unsatisfactory, you must have a local veterinarian examine it.

These certificates do some good, but most of them are a waste of the shipper's money. Those I have made out have done no more than state that I have examined the dog and found it to be in sound health and free from an infectious or communicable disease. I am not required to examine the dog's stools for parasites. Surely there is no way that I can tell if it is incubating a disease or has recently been infected; so by the time it arrives at its destination it may be blossoming with symptoms.

You will find the same situation at dog shows. Veterinarians examine the dogs, but they cannot possibly determine whether or not the dogs are incubating diseases. Many times my dogs have contracted Carré's disease at dog shows. No one is responsible. But it is possible to detect coccidiosis and all kinds of intestinal parasites by fecal examinations. This should be a part of every health examination. Obviously it is not, judging by the heavily infested dogs and puppies regularly being shipped from state to state.

So when you buy by mail you may buy a sick dog—one infested with parasites, one incubating a disease, or one that contracts a disease while in the hands of the transportation agency.

When buying this way you must be most specific in having certain requirements met. Since you can't see the dog and examine it for physical defects, you must ask questions in your letter, and state your requirements. Make a check list and send it. Here is a good sample:

The dog must have good vision.

The dog's parents must both have normal vision.

The dog must have perfect jaws, neither overshot nor undershot.

The dog must have dark eyes (if his breed is dark-eyed).

The dog must have both testicles in his scrotum.

Remember that the United States Post Office has rigid rules about using the mails to defraud, and if the description of the dog has been sent through the mail and is fraudulent, you can consult the Postal Inspector in your area, and he can be of great help to you. No one likes to be barred from using the mails, especially a dog dealer who sells his dogs that way.

If you are not confident that a dealer is one hundred percent reliable, or if you are suspicious that he or she is kennel-blind, you can very easily ask, at the time of your prospective purchase, a veterinarian to write out his opinion of physical soundness, freedom from obvious hereditary defects, and temperamental abnormalities as well as whether or not the dog is, in his judgment, purebred. This can be sent to you by airmail, and only after this opinion has been received would you give word to forward your dog.

Needless to say, this procedure requires that the dealer hold the dog for a few extra days, but the health certificate is good for that period of time or longer. Veterinarians can make mistakes in the matter of incubating diseases, but none can overlook the fact that a dog snapped at him when he was administering rabies vaccine or taking a temperature reading. He cannot miss discovering cryptorchidism, blindness, undershot or overshot animals, and unless he is inexperienced, he must know the physical appearances of the breeds. If dealers understand that these defects can so easily be discovered they would not bother to offer defective dogs for sale.

It is much more satisfactory to have descriptions in writing rather than by telephone. I have, on several occasions, been badly cheated by phone purchases and had no recourse because there was nothing on paper.

BUYING A TRAINED HUNTING DOG

We have been discussing buying dogs other than trained hunting dogs. If you are interested in one of these, be it a coonhound, foxhound, rabbit hound or bird dog of any breed, there are some facts you should know which may save you money.

In the first place, you can't always tell from reading an advertisement what kind of person is making the sale. The hunting dog field has many persons called "dog jockeys." Some are completely reliable, but some are not entirely trustworthy.

There are men who personally go out to buy and sell, and there are others who employ agents to buy for them. These agents go to rural towns, get all the information they can about the available dogs, phone in to describe them, and if the boss says "buy," they buy.

There are men in the business who, in the aggregate, have shipped hundreds of thousands of hounds. They sell for fairly high prices, and usually, these men buy carefully, but of course they expect many dogs to be returned. The dogs shipped are guaranteed to satisfy the buyer, but the buyer may live in a deer-infested area while the hound may have come from a section with no deer. Such a dog will be returned, fed, and sent out again and again, until he satisfies or gets lost.

The seller doesn't take much risk except with his reputation. He sells on six to ten days' trial. You, the buyer, pay express both ways. The reliable men give you trial from the time the dog arrives at your station, the less reliable from the time the dog was shipped. The latter may thus actually permit you only one night to try the dog. They have been under pretty close surveillance by the Post Office Department. Several have been fined heavily—one was fined five thousand dollars and refused the use of the mails.

Bird dog jockeys are fewer. The bird season is too short for many round trips of dogs for trial. Most bird dogs come from reliable trainers and not from dealers.

THE DOG POUND

There are those experienced with dogs, as well as those who feel they can't afford to buy one, who realize that often an excellent dog may be obtained from the dog pound or the kennel of the "Society-with-the-long-name."

Dog pounds are greatly improved compared with those of a generation ago. Before the advent of vaccines, any dog recovered by the pound, or taken from it, was almost certain to contract one or more diseases to which he had been exposed while there. There are still pounds like this in America, but in the more progressive areas the picture has changed. Some pounds are so well equipped and cared for that they rival veterinary hospitals and personal kennels.

If you want a dog that will not be costly, it may pay you to visit your local pound and inspect the conditions. Always keep in mind the fact that no one—no one—can tell you if a dog is incubating one or more diseases. The most immaculately kept dog pound must be suspect in this regard.

In the country there is quite a different situation. Frequently the dog warden is a farmer who has no patience with dogs that have unreliable dispositions, that piddle, and so forth. When the legal five days of confinement are up, he destroys such dogs and buries them. Those he keeps, hoping someone will call for a nice dog, are often quite reliable. It is far safer to look for a dog in a country pound than in a city or suburban one.

The same may be true in city kennels of the Society for the Prevention of Cruelty to Animals, or the Humane Society as many of them are now called. There are generally more individual kennel stalls on their premises, and the animals are given better care than in the average pound. The management seeks to find homes for good dogs rather than simply to comply with the law—to keep the dog the prescribed number of days and then destroy it to make room for another.

Don't expect that the dog will be given to you. Make a contribution of five or ten dollars to the Humane Society and, in all fairness, more if you can afford it later on when you find the dog is satisfactory. To the pound keeper you pay the amount prescribed by law. It may be three or five dollars.

Having obtained several outstanding dogs from both city and country pounds, my experience leads me to suggest that, if you obtain one from any of these agencies, you should do the following:

Take the dog home and try it. You can always return it if it is unsatisfactory. Don't permit yourself to become fond of the dog until you are certain that it is satisfactory. Don't expect it to be a model, housebroken puppy. Don't return it simply because it needs training; consider what great fun and satisfaction you will have while teaching it.

Keep the dog in isolation to determine whether he is incubating any disease. If after a week he is still healthy and has had no contact with neighborhood dogs, you can be reasonably sure he is not going to show symptoms of Carré's disease, hardpad disease, canine hepatitis, or leptospirosis—the four dangerous infectious diseases often contracted in pounds. Only rabies is still a problem. If you live in an area where none has been reported for a year, you need not worry that the new dog will develop symptoms.

At this point you should visit a veterinarian in whom you have confidence and have a fecal examination made. Have him deworm the dog, and vaccinate against as many diseases as possible—certainly against all of the four I mentioned and rabies as well.

At home, keep the dog isolated for another week, and he will not be likely to trouble you with illness. Observe his stools for tapeworm segments. If he has the kind which are contracted from fleas, your veterinarian is unlikely to discover their eggs when he makes his examination, but you will see segments which seem like grains of rice in the stool, sometimes under his tail, and even in his bed. Tell the D.V.M. and let him deworm the dog, especially if you have small children, because sometimes a child will swallow a flea which has eaten tapeworm eggs and become infected.

As a final word on obtaining a pet, don't expect to buy a cheap puppy and think you can overcome its poor heredity by training. You can't, although many persons think so. And don't buy a dog with bad habits. You may be able to brainwash and train the dog correctly, but first ask yourself: Is it worth it? Remember the results with the "detrained" army attack dogs. Of those I knew, each one had to be watched and restrained constantly. And these were carefully selected dogs, not the real tough characters. Special trainers spent a great deal of time and patience "detraining" them too.

ADDITIONAL EXPENSES

Consider any further expenses you may have, such as the following examples. Have you decided on a boxer, Doberman pinscher, or Great Dane whose ears have yet to be cropped? This costs between $10 and $25, plus a lot of trouble. Has the puppy's tail been docked? If the pup is a spaniel or a terrier, it should have been done by the time he was six days old. Does the puppy have unsightly extra toes (dewclaws) on his hind legs? Unless he is a water dog, they should have been removed in his first few days of life. If these operations have not been performed, add their cost to the purchase price of your pet.

Buy inexpensive paraphernalia for a puppy, because he'll outgrow it quickly. Wait until the dog is adult, then buy good, durable accessories for him.

If you select your dog or puppy carefully, the chances are you will be amply rewarded for your thought, time, and trouble.

REGISTRATION

There seems to be so much confusion over the terms *pedigree, papers, licensed,* and *registered* that you should know what they mean.

A *pedigree* is a sheet of paper with the names of the close ancestors of the puppy written on it in chart form. You can have a pedigree chart of a mongrel with eight breeds in its make-up or of a purebred dog whose ancestors were all of the same breed.

Papers may mean pedigree or registration certificate. The term is too loose and is frequently used to deceive unsuspecting people. If you are offered *papers,* ask what the papers represent.

Licensed is a purely local appellation. You pay your town clerk for a license to keep a dog. In some states the license is given out by other agencies—the veterinarian who immunizes your dog against rabies in some southern states. You get your dog's license, in New York City, from the A.S.P.C.A.

Registration papers are just the proof that your dog's parents were registered in one of the several registry organizations in the world. In the United States there is The American Kennel Club, 51 Madison Avenue, New York, New York, the largest of such organizations, which registers more breeds than any other.

The American Field, 222 West Adams Street, Chicago, Ill., chiefly registers bird-hunting breeds. Many of the family records of great field-trial pointers and setters are kept in its files. The organization also registers many other breeds.

The United Kennel Club, Kalamazoo, Mich., registers most of the coonhound, mountain lion, and bearhound breeds, also smooth fox terriers, fighting bulldogs (pit bulls), farm shepherds, spitz, and others.

The Chase Studbook, Lexington, Ky., registers foxhounds mainly, but coonhounds and some other breeds as well.

The racing greyhound breeders have their own association, and there are others, such as the A.H.A. (American Hound Association).

If a breeder or dealer tells you your puppy is a purebred and eligible for registration, he may be referring to any of the above organizations.

Most of these organizations insist first that each litter of puppies be registered. The litter is given a number. The breeder then fills out a blank for the individual registration of each puppy in the litter and one goes with each puppy. When you want your dog registered you send this application, completed with your signature and agreement to abide by the rules, to the registering association together with the fee which is printed on the application. If the paper is properly filled out and the name you have chosen to be your dog's registered name is not a duplicate of another, you will be issued a registration certificate. If you want a nicely typed pedigree you may have it from the American Kennel Club for a special fee, and some of the registry organizations send it as part of the first fee.

The American Kennel Club has a rule of special interest to every dog buyer: if a puppy is entitled to be registered, the papers must accompany it unless there is a written agreement between the seller and the buyer that the puppy is sold and bought without a registration application. The purpose of this rule is to prevent dishonest dealers and breeders from passing off unregistered dogs as eligible when they are not.

If a breeder or dealer says to you, "The price on this pup is twenty dollars without A.K.C. papers and forty dollars with," you may be pretty sure it has no right to papers. If you return after the puppy is grown and offer the breeder the twenty dollars for the "papers," the chances are he can't furnish them. It costs him only two dollars to register the whole litter. Why should he ask you twenty dollars for one application, properly signed?

If the seller of your dog tells you it has papers or a pedigree, or is licensed, now that you know what these terms mean, you won't be content unless he shows you the litter registration or assures you that the dog is eligible for registration in one of the several associations. He may have sent the application in and not yet received the registration. Sometimes this process takes three months, so patience is needed.

When you decide to keep the dog you must send the individual registration application to the registry association. It may be several months also before you receive the final certificate.

How then can you be sure you are buying a purebred dog? If you are not sufficiently experienced to know what one looks like, you must either rely on the honor of the seller or get an expert to look at the puppy for you. There are instances when the most expert dog man cannot tell. And there are other cases where the breeder is inexperienced and doesn't know how a purebred puppy of the breed he fancies should look. Neophyte breeders often register litters of mongrels as purebreds, unaware that the dam has been mated to a dog of another breed.

Chapter Three

THE BREEDS TODAY AS I SEE THEM

There are so many wonderful dogs available that there's a good one for every person willing to study his own requirements and find the dog to suit him. In this chapter you will find my table of breed characteristics as well as a description of certain breeds that are sometimes overlooked. Frequently the best dog for a particular owner or family is not among those currently in style.

TABLE OF BREED CHARACTERISTICS

Of more than one hundred breeds of dogs in America, I have, in the following chart, listed only the most popular. Popularity is, of course, no criterion of quality; there are many excellent breeds whose worth still needs to be generally recognized. The chart lists the basic characteristics of 47 breeds; it is designed as a starting point to aid in your selection of a dog.

ORIGIN OF BREEDS

In the long run a frank acknowledgment of faults is good for any breed. As long as German shepherd breeders, for example, insist that their dogs have universally "sweet dispositions," why alter them? Only by acknowledging the disagreeable features can they be eliminated through careful selective breeding.

The British breeds are the most numerous. They are the most evenly bred and typed and are tops in temperament because English breeders value temperament so highly. Voices are usually pleasant. Types tend toward exaggeration. They will not be listed as are the other breeds by nationality because there are so many.

Breeds of American Origin

Coonhounds: Redbone, Black-and-tan (medium ears); Black-and-tan (long ears); Plott; Bluetick; English: Treeing Walker

Foxhounds: Walker; Trigg; Birdsong; Black-and-tan

American Bloodhound

Field Trial Pointers

Field Trial Setters

Cocker Spaniel

Woolly Cocker Spaniel

Chesapeake Bay Retriever

Fox Terrier

Boston Terrier

American Shepherd

Toy Boxer

By and large the American breeds are excellent performers. They are the least expensive of the breeds when puppies, and the most expensive when trained. They do their jobs better than many European dogs, but because they are younger breeds, they are perhaps not as uniform. In temperament they are generally excellent.

Breeds of German Origin

German Short-haired Pointer

Dachshund

Schnauzer: Giant; Standard; Miniature

German Shepherd

Doberman Pinscher

Boxer

Great Dane

Pomeranian

Dalmatian

Weimaraner

KEY: THE NUMBER OF X'S INDICATES THE DEGREE OF EACH TRAIT. ONE X MEANS LEAST; FOUR X'S MEAN MOST.

	AVERAGE WEIGHT	DAILY FOOD COSTS	GROOMING REQUIREMENTS	SAFE, RELIABLE TEMPERAMENT	DIFFICULTY OF HOUSEBREAKING	DESTRUCTIVENESS AS PUPPIES	FIDGETINESS	BOISTEROUSNESS	SUSCEPTIBILITY TO SKIN DISEASE	PLEASANT QUALITY OF VOICE	GOOD FOR APARTMENTS	GOOD AS CHILDREN'S PETS	TENDENCY TO: FIGHT	ROAM	BARK	DIG	GO INTO WATER	HERD
Terriers																		
Airedale	60	16	XX	XX	x		x		XXX	X	XX	XX	XXX	XXX	x		x	
Wirehair	18	6	x	XX	XX	x	XX	XX	x	x	XXXX	XXX	XX	XXX	XXX	XXX	x	
Dachshund	20	7	x	XX	XXX	XXX	XXX	x	x	x	XXXX	XXX	XX	XXX	XXX	XX	x	
Boston	20	7	XX	XX	XX	XXX			x	XX	XXXX	XXX	XX	XXX	XXX	XX	x	
Irish	40	11	x	XX	XX	XX	XXX	x	XX	XX	XXXX	XXX	XX	XXX	XXX	XXXX	XX	
Am. smooth fox 18.	18	6	x	XXX	XX	x	XX	XX	x	x	XXXX	XXX	XX	XX	XX	XX	x	
Eng. smooth fox	20	7	x	XXX	XX	XX	XX	XX	x	x	XXXX	XXX	XX	XX	XX	x	x	
Welsh	20	7	XXX	XXX	XX	XX			XX	XX	XXXX	XXX	XX	x	x	XXX	x	
Scottish	30	9	XXX	XXX	XXX	x		x	XXXX	x	XXXX	XXXX	XX	x	x	XXX	x	
Sealyham	30	9	XXX	XXX	XXX		x		XXXX	XX	XXXX	XXXX	XX	x	x	XXX	x	
Shepherds																		
Am. farm	55	15	XX	XXX	x	x			XXXX	XX	XXXX	XXXX	x	x	x	XX	x	XXXX
Collie	60	16	XX	XXX	x	x		x	XX	x	XX	XXX	x	XX	x	x	x	XXX
Shetland sheep dog	35	10	XX	XXX	XX	x	x		XX	XX	XXXX	XXXX	x	x	x		x	XXX

Breed	Average Weight	Daily Food Costs	Grooming Requirements	Safe, Reliable Temperament	Difficulty of Housebreaking	Destructiveness as Puppies	Fidgetiness	Boisterousness	Susceptibility to Skin Disease	Pleasant Quality of Voice	Good for Apartments	Good as Children's Pets	Tendency to: Fight	Tendency to: Roam	Tendency to: Bark	Tendency to: Dig	Tendency to: Go Into Water	Tendency to: Herd
Spaniels																		
Am. cocker	25 lb.	8¢	XXX	XX	XX				XX	XX	XXX	XX	X	X	XX		XXX	
Eng. cocker	35	10	XX	XXXX	X	X			XX	XX	XXX	XX	XX	X	X		XXX	
Springer	45	12	XX	XX	XX	XX	X	X	XX	XX	XXX	XXX	X	XX	XX	XX	XXXX	
Setters																		
English	60	16	XX	XXX	XX	X			X	X	XX	XX	X	XX	XX		XXX	
Irish	60	16	XX	XX	XX	XXX		X	X	X	XX	XX	XX	XXXX	XX		XX	
Gordon	65	17	XX	XXX	XX	X	X	X	X	XXXX	XX	XX	X	XXXX	XX		XX	
Hounds (Scent)																		
Fox and Coon	55	15	XX	XXX	XX	X	X		X	X	X	XXXX	X	XXXX	XXX	XX	XXX	
Beagle	20	7	X	XXX	XX	XX		X	X	X	X	XX	XX	XX	XXX	XX	X	
Hounds (Sight)																		
Greyhound	50	14	X	XX	XXX	XX			X	X	XXX	X	XXX	XX	X			
Rus. wolfhound	60	16	XX	XX	XXX		X		X	X	XXXX	X	XX	XX	X			
Bulldogs																		
English	45	12	X	XXX	XX	XX			X	XX	XXX	XX	XXXX	XX	X	XX		
French	20	7	X	XXX	XX	XX		XX	X	X	XXX	XXX	XX	X	X			
Bull terrier	40	11	X	XXX	X	XXX		X		XX	XXX	XXX	XXX	XX	X		X	

Group / Breed		
Watchdogs		
Boxer	65	17
Ger. shepherd	80	20
Doberman pinscher	75	19
Norwegian elkhound	55	15
Dalmatian	55	15
Spitz	30	9
Chow	45	12
Toys		
Chihuahua	5	3
Pomeranian	7	4
Pekingese	12	5
Pug	16	6
Giants		
Saint Bernard	130	25
Newfoundland	120	24
Great Dane	110	23
Ir. wolfhound	150	35
Retrievers		
Golden	60	16
Chesapeake Bay	65	17
Labrador	60	16
Poodles		
Standard	55	15
Miniature	20	7
Pointer	55	15

The German breeds sent directly from Germany are the least reliable in temperament. With the exception of the German short-haired pointer, they are less competent workers, although superb watch dogs. German breeds, however, such as dachshunds, Alsatians, and Great Danes, kept by the British for some canine generations and then brought to America have quite reliable temperaments.

CLASSIFICATION OF BREEDS

Dog owners, for many years, have been confused by an absurd A.K.C. classification of breeds. One large class is called the Non-Sporting Group. No one seems to know what this means; yet no one seems to have the temerity to challenge it, much less to change it. So it goes on and on. Toys of course are non-sporting (although not listed in this A.K.C. classification), and working dogs are non-sporting. Terriers kept as pets and watchdogs are in similar "non-sporting" groups. Really an absurd division of dogdom!

I am proposing a classification based on the dog's use to man. It won't please everyone, but I've yet to discuss it with any open-minded person who failed to agree.

One of the good features of the following classification is that it transcends all registry associations, bringing together for the first time all of the breeds in America.

There is one fact you must remember—when a dog is a genuine toy it is a midget. The dwarfing which causes this diminution does something more than simply shrink the size; it changes the character. Such dogs are only suited for pets. By the same token giantism also has the effect of making dogs of very little use except as breed curiosities. Great Dane breeders can tell you how the Dane was once a boarhound. When he was, he was probably no giant but a powerful, agile dog capable of fast running and endurance. Most of the present-day Danes are too cumbersome for such work. St. Bernards, developed at the Hospice of St. Bernard, certainly did not have to be giants to locate lost persons—a Grahund with its dense coat would probably do a better job. Giants have little endurance and tend to be short-lived. The only really big dog I know of that has any real endurance is the Irish wolfhound, and it is doubtful that the largest of them can keep going as well as the smaller.

So here I place giants together, because that's all they are now—curiosities, despite their old-time value. One can't classify them as guards because they are not sufficiently alert. Some find it an effort even to get to their feet. The giants are really dogs for persons who fancy oddities, just as a person may fancy pouter pigeons.

It isn't necessary to spend "vast sums on food," as one man put it when he was showing how valuable they are. The largest giant dog, say one weighing two hundred and fifty pounds (which was the heaviest I ever saw), can be well fed for under thirty-five cents a day.

My Classification of the Breeds:

Scent Hounds

Fox hounds: Walker; Long-eared Black-and-tan; Birdsong; Trigg; English; Harrier
Tree Hounds: Redbone; Plott; Medium-eared Black-and-tan; Long-eared Black-and-tan; English; Bluetick

Bloodhound
Basset Hound
Beagle
Otterhound
Rhodesian Ridgeback

Sight Hounds

Greyhound
Whippet

Irish Wolfhound
Borzoi

Afghan   Saluki
Scottish Deerhound

The Bird Dog Breeds

UPLAND BIRD DOGS

Pointer   Brittany Spaniel
American Pointer   Irish Setter
English Setter (show type)   German Short-haired Pointer
English Setter (shooting type)   Weimaraner
English Setter (field-trial type)   Vizsla
Gordon Setter   Wire-haired Pointing Griffon

SPANIELS

American Cocker Spaniel   English Springer Spaniel
English Cocker Spaniel   Welsh Springer Spaniel
American Water Spaniel   Clumber Spaniel
Field Spaniel   Sussex Spaniel

RETRIEVERS

Chesapeake Bay Retriever   Labrador Retriever (black)
Curly-coated Retriever   Labrador Retriever (yellow)
Flat-coated Retriever   Irish Water Spaniel
Golden Retriever

TERRIERS

American Fox Terrier   Bedlington Terrier
English Fox Terrier (smooth-   Dandie Dinmont Terrier
  coated)   Skye Terrier
English Fox Terrier (wire-   West Highland White Terrier
  coated)   Manchester Terrier
Airedale   Dachshund (short-coated)
Kerry Blue Terrier   Dachshund (wire-coated)
Irish Terrier   Dachshund (long-coated)
Lakeland Terrier   Border Terrier
Welsh Terrier   Staffordshire Terrier
Norwich Terrier   Australian Terrier
Cairn Terrier   Affenpinscher
Scottish Terrier   Standard Schnauzer
Sealyham Terrier   Miniature Schnauzer

SHEPHERD DOGS

American Farm Shepherd
Collie (smooth)
Collie (rough)
Border Collie
Shetland Sheepdog
Cardigan Welsh Corgi

Pembroke Welsh Corgi
Belgian Sheepdog
Puli
Komondor
Kuvasz
Bernese Mountain Dog

GUARD AND ATTACK DOGS

Mastiff
Bull Mastiff
Bull Terrier (white)
Bull Terrier (colored)
German Shepherd (Alsatian Wolfdog)
Doberman Pinscher
Boxer

Schipperke
Giant Schnauzer
Rottweiler
Keeshond
Briard
Bouvier des Flanders
Chow Chow

BULLDOGS

Bulldog

French Bulldog

NORTHERN AND SLED DOGS

Wolf
Alaskan Malemute
Grahund (Norwegian Elkhound)
Alghund

Eskimo
Samoyed
Siberian Husky

GIANT DOGS

Great Dane
St. Bernard (rough-coated)
St. Bernard (smooth-coated)

Newfoundland
Great Pyrenees

TOY DOGS

Pekingese
Pomeranian
Toy Poodle
Toy Boxer

Japanese Spaniel
Papillon
Yorkshire Terrier
Toy Manchester

Chihuahua (short-coated)	Maltese
Chihuahua (long-coated)	Italian Greyhound
Blenheim Spaniel	Brussels Griffon
Prince Charles Spaniel	Miniature Pinscher
King Charles Spaniel	Mexican Hairless
Ruby Spaniel	Lhasa Apso

"YOU NAME IT"

(The proper classification of these dogs will require considerable study.)

Standard Poodle	Boston Terrier
Miniature Poodle	Pug
Dalmatian	Basenji

HOUNDS

Beagle

People are having more fun with beagles today than with any other breed of dog. It stands near the top in A.K.C. registrations, and its rise in popularity has been rapid and steady. Part of this increase has been due to the disillusionment of cocker spaniel owners who found themselves troubled with the extensive grooming required by the modern woolly cockers. Beagles have proved to be the size wanted, without the disadvantages of ultra-long, ultra-thick hair. This is a partial explanation of the beagle's enormous popularity.

Most of the gain, however, came from the field-trial boys who know how to have fun with dogs. Beagle field trials are second in number only to the coonhound trials.

Beagles generally have even, gentle dispositions. They are inexpensive, and the breeders have no compunction about destroying ill-tempered individuals and those that do not perform as they should when hunting rabbits. All over the United States one finds small packs of beagles where a bird-dog enthusiast or a coon hunter may only keep his individual dog.

Few are the rabbit hunters who are content to own one beagle. There are hundreds of clubs each with its clubhouse or meeting place, and each club holds several field trials every year, some for amateurs and some for professionals.

The little dogs are bred in several sizes, or classes as they are called, and are measured in inches at the shoulder. Thus there are nine-, eleven-, thirteen- and fifteen-inch classes. The number of people exhibiting beagles in shows is increasing, but still is relatively small.

If beagles have any fault it is that they like to roam, and of course, they love to hunt. I've heard a few people complain that neighbors' dogs annoyed them by barking on rabbit tracks in suburban areas. Their intense interest in pursuing game can also lead them to cross roads without regard to automobiles.

The overall picture of this breed is one of merry, good-natured, satisfactory little dogs, as yet quite unspoiled, which have deservedly won their way into the hearts of thousands of Americans. President Johnson's two pets Him and Her, and the famous ear-pulling incident have helped to increase their popularity.

Foxhound

In England, "riding to the hounds" used to be the prerogative of the upper class where everyone was taught to hunt. As a result of this widespread interest, probably the finest hound known was developed. For this purpose it had to be a *pack* hound, since once the fox was sighted, the dogs were taught to pursue it as a group.

In time, the English foxhound became a uniform breed with heavy straight legs, shortish necks, stout construction and wonderfully expressive eyes. The color was generally white, black, and tan. The dogs were housed in packs, not in separate kennels and got along together admirably. They were not eager to fight, but, once in a contest, proved formidable antagonists.

The English foxhounds were brought to America in the early colonial days. There are a few packs of these dogs in England and America, but the American packs are slowly becoming American, having few of the typical English fox-hounds among them.

Among the early hounds were mavericks—dogs that chose not to "pack." These were crossed with bloodhounds which are also individualists. The result was the American long-eared black-and-tan foxhound. This was and is a real fox-hound used individually by a single hunter.

Fox hides were an important item of the fur industry, and each hound would start his fox and run it. A fox makes great circles, often many miles in diameter. The hunter "took his stand" (sat on a stump, perhaps) and waited. The beautiful booming voice of his hound told him that the fox would be along soon. Sometimes a hound possessed such a methodical steady bay that the fox lost his fear of the pursuer, regarding the dog as a mere nuisance and trotted along only fifty yards ahead. The chase might go on for twenty-four or thirty-six hours, dog and fox covering hundreds of miles, but eventually the hunter's gun ended the chase, and the fox was skinned.

This was the great American hound which today is regis-tered by the A.K.C. as the black-and-tan coonhound. There are still some who hunt foxes with them but since the price of fox pelts shrank from twenty-five dollars to twenty-five cents, the incentive to hunt them was gone. Now the price of fox pelts has risen. Will the hound come back to greater popularity?

At the same time that this magnificent animal was in his prime, the Southern hunters were developing another kind of foxhound. This was the competitive type exemplified by the

Walker, a Kentucky breed. A large number of breeds or strains are hunted principally at night. The fox is as sacred to the Southern hunter as he is in England. Never shoot a fox!

From this kind of fox hunting the field trial developed and spread all over America. The vast fox hunting fraternity is catered to by three excellent magazines.

City persons may know about the small numbers of fox hunting clubs whose members ride to the hounds, but the total number of dogs in them is not to be compared with the thousands of these great backwoods dogs. The A.K.C. registered just fifty of them in 1965; The International Fox Hunters' Stud Book and other associations take care of them, but only a few of the total are ever registered. I'm not recommending a foxhound as a pet unless you live where you can use him. If you can, it won't be long before you have more than one, and your life will be immeasurably fuller.

Coonhound

Among the most popular of all the breeds in America are these country dogs which are almost unknown to city people. Most of the real coonhounds are registered in the U.K.C. The A.K.C. registers the long-eared, black-and-tan coonhound, but in the opinion of most of the hunters I know, these are really foxhounds. The ears are much too long for practical coon hunting.

The U.K.C. registers a hound with intermediate-length ears, black-and-tan in color, which is the practical dog for the job.

Although there are six coonhound breeds, I am reasonably sure that the day is coming when there will be only two. As I have repeatedly watched the judging at U.K.C. shows, I have been impressed that the chief difference between some of the breeds is coloring only. The coon hunters will not like to read this, but I think they (or we) would do well to have an American coonhound, whose breed would be divided into color classes. Thus there would be a black-and-tan class, a red class, a white-spotted class, a bluetick class, and a brindle. The respective present names for these classes are black-and-tan, Redbone, Treeing Walker, English, and Plott. In addition to this American coonhound breed, I would have the bluetick which is much more bulky and bloodhoundy than the more lithe, trim, and agile dogs of the other strains.

Bloodhound (English and American)

This breed, mentioned so often, despite its scarcity, is known for its perseverance. In America it has found its greatest field of usefulness, and "bloodhound detectives" have used their dogs successfully in thousands of instances—capturing criminals, finding lost persons, and even locating the dead.

The bloodhound has proved to be one of the most useful of dogs. Although only a few are registered in the A.K.C., there are many doing yeoman work whose parents or grandparents were not registered. In contrast to the heavy phlegmatic English type, an agile, efficient American type is evolving. Neither type of bloodhound is a house dog but they are wonderful companions.

The bloodhound's skin is loose, his ears are fairly long but not like those of the black-and-tan foxhound. His disposition is even and easygoing until he goes to work on the trail. This is where he shines, and a man must be in good condition to hold his leash.

Basset Hound

It is regrettable that Gerald Livingston, the man who kept the basset going in America for years and years, is not living to see what great popularity television has brought the breed.

There may be mean bassets but I've never seen one. They

are generally hunted in packs, but from my own experience I cannot see that they do as well as beagles, for they become exhausted too soon for all-day hunters. The bloodhound-basset crosses did have tremendous endurance, but they did not run in jumps as many bassets do.

Unless you dislike the short legs, you will go far to find a finer house pet than a basset. Those I have known were quite long-lived, which is an especially important consideration in buying a dog. The short, smooth coat and silky ears make them pleasant to handle and easy to care for, and they leave little hair about when they shed.

Greyhound

There are forty thousand or more greyhounds in the U.S.A. Do you think it strange you see so few as pets? If you knew the breed, you would not wonder. Greyhounds have been bred with only one object in mind—to turn out dogs that can win races. What does that require? A "sweet disposition"? A nice, quiet dog that doesn't love to roam? A comfortable dog to have around? A greyhound can, and often does, have an even, reliable temperament; he may be quiet and comfortable to have around, but that's not what he has been bred for all these years. He runs on a track in a muzzle, and he is strictly a kennel dog. He is possessed of an almost irresistible impulse to chase anything that moves, which makes them difficult pets. Many discards from tracks *are* adopted by families (I had a dandy once), but they often run blindly into the paths of autos while pursuing some neighbor's cat or dog.

Although not very satisfactory pets, greyhounds are among the very best dogs ever created for their work—to chase and kill rabbits, foxes, coyotes, and even timber wolves. They work in pairs or packs. They are quick as lightning with their slashing bites and usually kill a hare with one snap.

The greyhounds you see in shows are usually the picture

variety kept for shows and registered in the A.K.C. The greyhounds you see at the tracks are bred for speed; it makes little difference how they look. They are part of a million-dollar business involving owners, gamblers, tracks, and the states where racing is permitted. It's remarkable that their dispositions are so reliable.

Whippet

What I have said about greyhounds applies to whippets, except that more whippets than greyhounds are bred for show and registered in the A.K.C. Quite a lot are kept as pets, probably because of their exquisite beauty. They are statuesque to look at in repose or in action.

Whippet races are fun. They are less than half the length of greyhound races and are run on a straight track. Many persons find that breeding them to combine speed and temperament is rewarding. I would not recommend one for a family with young children. He would not take kindly to having his tail pulled or ears tweaked.

Afghan Hound

The Afghan hound is a showpiece, and many consider it the most aristocratic of all the breeds. When the attractive Sunny Shay takes one flying along the beach, it is a magnificent spectacle. The temperaments of most are excellent, although I knew one strain that was vicious.

The Afghan requires an enormous amount of care. If you buy one, do so with your eyes wide open. The hair is silky and mats and tangles constantly. One burr tangled in the coat needs many minutes of combing; with many burrs you have clip the dog all over. To use one for hunting anywhere but in a bushless desert, it would have to be clipped.

As a showpiece for those with unlimited leisure, an Afghan

can afford great satisfaction. And if you want to attract attention, girls, get one. It is so showy, however, that the men may wolf whistle at the dog rather than at you.

BIRD DOGS

English Setter

Even if you wanted to find faults, it would be difficult. The English dog is a beautiful creation with a saintly disposition, which at its proper work—hunting upland birds—is a masterpiece of loveliness. As one bird hunter remarked, after seeing his dog point a pheasant when the bird rose ahead of it, feathers glistening in the morning sunlight; "For that one ten-second experience and the memory of the picture, it would be worth keeping the dog in my kennel for a whole year."

The English is the slower, close-working dog favored by thousands. From this type, Americans have developed the field-trial dog which runs so fast and so wide that trials are generally conducted on horseback, as in the case of pointers that compete with the setters. That there has been much promiscuous crossing of these breeds no one can doubt, especially when one finds liver-and-white setters and long-haired and tricolored pointers appearing in litters of so-called purebreds. Today it is difficult to find intermediate working English setters because of the fetish of breeding to field-trial winners. One is faced with the choice between the more beautiful and ponderous English type and the quick, fast American.

Gordon or Black-and-Tan Setter

The Gordon is a great personal favorite with many as a beautiful hunting dog, but it is seldom entered in the big field trials.

Irish

The Irish is a roamer, owners say, and he develops little allegiance to any one person. He is not much of a watch dog. The English and the Gordon are preferred by those who know the three types as companions and house dogs.

The coats of all three are flat against the body and need only occasional combing to keep in shape. The belly hair, the long hair on the tail, and the feathers on the backs of the legs comb out quite easily. Why aren't more setters kept as pets? Fashion seems not to have decreed it. If you don't care about owning a popular breed, look into setters, even if you do not hunt birds. When you get it, go and watch some field-trial competition, and be sure to take your camera loaded with color film.

Pointer

There are several kinds of pointers. The pointer and the German short-haired pointer are well known, but today we also have the American pointer, even if he is not yet recognized as a breed. Many persons still cherish the illusion that the pointer is a Spanish dog, but research indicates that there was an English dog not too different from the present English pointer long before any Spanish dog was brought to that country. In fact, all over Europe there seem to have been short-haired bird hunting dogs.

The components that went into the production of the breed were foxhound, greyhound, and setter. The bird interest is exceedingly dominant, and it must have been easy to weed out the less capable dogs.

In America we still have the close-hunting English strain, but the breed is rapidly becoming a high-tailing, exceedingly fast-running, wide-ranging type. Persons wanting pointers usually buy dogs from noted field-trial specimens—the dogs that win the big events, and the big events are run where they ride horses to keep up with the dogs.

Pointers are winning more of these events than are setters. While there has been considerable mixture of the two in the past, the pointer still retains a different, harder temperament. He is a better guard dog than the setter. He has a competitive spirit and tremendous endurance. His points, which are probably hypnotic, tend to last for long periods if the dog is not found. Having short hair, he is preferred in cover that abounds in burrs.

Some say pointers are hardheaded, and trainers who claim that this is true are pleased, because when the dog is finally trained, he is just as hardheaded in losing what he has learned and performs better.

Before the dog was bred for severe field work in the U.S.A., I think he was a better home dog than he is today. Today, outside of bird-hunting territory, few pointers are kept as pets though it is quite possible that certain strains will become popular as house dogs again.

German Short-Haired Pointer

The German short-haired pointer has gained in popularity because in America it has been quickly adapted to our conditions, and it has earned an "A" both for natural innate ability and for effort. Unfortunately, like so many other German imports, it was handicapped by being introduced as a general-purpose dog. Because the originators, we are told, had "infused" bloodhounds, foxhounds, the pointers into the composite animal, it was supposed to be a man trailer, a hound, etc. The ticking in its color makes one suspect that some good English setters were also used. In fact, it is really an English dog in the same way that most of our American breeds are

English, but the "short-hair" was selected for German bird-hunting conditions. It is *not* a general-purpose dog but a highly efficient bobtail bird dog, being a staunch pointer and excellent retriever. Duck hunters like the breed for retrieving, but I have never known one that was a really competent trailer. My impression is that for the toughest bird-hunting conditions it is certainly the equal of either our pointers or setters.

This is a very new breed, well mixed with others, so if you breed them, expect some variation in the litters for some generations to come. Most of the puppies are already quite uniform.

Weimaraner

If you want a buckskin-colored dog with yellow eyes and not much of anything else, buy one. It is not, as claimed, a proficient trail hound, but it is a fair bird dog. In time American breeders may make the breed first-class for upland bird hunting.

As yet it is quite unstable, sometimes producing black and even long-haired puppies. Its voice is not to be compared with that of a good Redbone which it resembles in body build. (Redbones sometimes produce buckskin-colored puppies which the owners destroy.)

Weimaraners once sold for three hundred dollars each, but now that the public is aware of their flaws, puppies frequently sell for only twenty-five dollars.

SPANIELS

American Cocker Spaniel

The American cocker spaniel first became popular in Canada. The breeders in the Boston area, many of them dog fanciers of long experience, recognized that it was an ideal little companion in the home and in the field, and entirely without exaggeration, they helped it climb in popularity. Their chief tool was honesty. I knew a lot of these people, and I spoke on numerous occasions to cocker groups and heard their discussions of the breed.

Sound temperament was basic in their selection. They put longer legs under the Canadian dogs, and when Idahurst Belle won best at "the Garden" the breed had reached its zenith. The breed reached a popularity never before attained by any other. One out of every four dogs registered in the A.K.C. was a cocker. Show classes—Black, Parti-colored, and A.S.C.O.B. (any solid color other than black).

Then commercialism, careless breeding, and practically no selection for temperament damaged the breed. To cap it all, there was the clique of breeders who, with the sanction of A.K.C., arranged it so that only cockers with huge, woolly, clipped coats had a Chinaman's chance of winning. That did it. Down went the breed in popularity because so few persons wanted such a dog.

What was the *real* American cocker like? It was twenty to twenty-four pounds with long hair on sides and back of legs (feather). The tail was docked. In color there was a wide choice, from fawn to black and from all white to solid color. The head was characterized by prominent soulful, expressive eyes, and by ears which hung low on the sides with a fringe of straight easily combed hair.

The proper cocker didn't know its teeth were made to bite. Being a retriever, one could catch a baby chick and not bite it. The dog hungered for human companionship, was never shy, and did not piddle when surprised or happy. And the breed was long-lived, many reached fifteen years in sound health.

Cocker spaniel field trials are becoming increasingly popular. The enthusiasts look with scorn on the woolly type and insist on sound temperaments. With this group as a nucleus, and with the other admirers of the unbarbered, natural, delightful cocker, I believe the breed will again achieve a well-warranted popularity. If I were a young man, I would try to find some of the old type and breed them. There is a great demand for them, but they are hard to find.

Woolly Cocker

Because this section of the book is written to help you choose the proper dog for yourself or family, we must discuss the present barbered cocker, a truly beautiful product of breeding and clipping. If you admire the cockers at the shows, remember that hours and hours have been spent grooming them. But picture one ungroomed, living in your home where it can run outside. You may live in the suburbs. Think what the long thick coat, almost dragging the ground, could pick up and bring inside! The modern cocker breeders are mostly wealthy persons who can turn the care of their dogs over to professionals to keep them in proper condition.

If you are determined to buy one, investigate carefully the temperament of the parents. Remember that dogs bred mostly for show need not be bred as household pets. There are still many cockers with as fine dispositions; your job will be to find one.

English Cocker Spaniel

It is strange how the English, the Canadian, and the American breeds have changed in recent years. Certainly they look sufficiently different to be two breeds. Unfortunately, the adverse publicity that was showered on the American breed, when the deserved reaction to careless breeding and woolly coats set in, affected the English dog too, even though he in no way deserved it.

The English cocker, given half a chance, is a wonderful dog. However, he is not yet sufficiently popular for every kennel to market dogs of uniform quality.

The coat needs no clipping; there are enough colors to satisfy any taste, and the temperaments are almost invariably sound.

Springer Spaniel

Talk about a general-purpose dog! The springer, although not advertised as such, comes nearer to this definition than any breed I know. Primarily, the springer is a water bird dog. It swims well, retrieves beautifully, sheds water quite well, and has the constitution to stand the cold. It is a grand dog for duck hunting.

But, in addition, it trails like a hound, and some bark on the trail. It makes a fine pheasant dog, is often used to hunt rabbits, and one is occasionally found that hunts coons.

Add to this the fact that this bird dog makes an excellent companion and house pet, and you see what I mean by "general-purpose" dog. It has a good temperament and will stand a lot of abuse. The only objection to it is the longish hair, but it still is not as difficult to groom as the woolly cocker.

Springers come in black-and-white and liver-and-white. The latter have yellow eyes, brown noses, and footpads. Of medium size, there are two types registered—the English and the Welsh, the ratio was 5863 to 28 in 1965.

Brittany Spaniel

This red-and-white French breed, midway in size between setter and spaniel, yet called a spaniel, is a real bird hunter's dog. I have known of several men, experts in bird hunting and widely experienced with all breeds of bird dogs, who felt it was the best they could buy. It is unlikely that you will see them kept as pets because, while they have sound temperaments and bird sense, there is little to recommend them as objects of beauty. Few who do not know the breed seem willing to believe that any individual specimen is anything but a mongrel. Still, they make splendid, if homely, companions.

Observe the old prints of bird dogs in action and you will find that many resemble the present-day Brittany spaniel except that their tails are natural, whereas the "Brits'" tails appear absent or, at most, about two inches long. The general type is quite ancient, but it is only a little over a century since the first naturally tailless pups were born and the breed was established. History tells us that the French used pointers and setters to cross with Brittanys at about the beginning of the century, and so this young breed is not too stable as yet. Why it is called a spaniel is difficult to understand for its natural behavior patterns place it squarely in the class of the upland bird dogs. It is fast, being improved to suit our hunting conditions, and for anyone wanting a smallish bobtailed setter that is an excellent gun dog and retriever, the Brittany can be recommended *if* it has been bred for hunting and not for show.

RETRIEVERS

As a group, retrievers have never been so popular that they have been ruined, either for the purpose for which they were developed or in temperament. On the whole the group is amazingly satisfactory and solid. The one United States native, the rusty-colored Chesapeake Bay retriever, has been kept as much as a watch dog as for retrieving birds. He has a little more of the Airedale temperament than any of the other retrievers—a lot of dog, powerful and forceful, but wonderful for his job. In the country, women like to have Chesapeakes because they are so protective. All the retrievers have thick coats.

The Labrador, black, and now yellow, has one of the most

even dispositions of any dog ever developed. Some persons object to their tendency to become overweight. They are also said to lack vivacity, but this is a trait which can soon become tiring. A Labrador will always light up when he is pleased, and I've never seen one that was a bundle of nerves.

The golden retriever is much like the Labrador. The coat is longer but not long enough to be difficult. I've worked with a great many and have yet to see the one that was not all that a dog should be.

You can have a retriever in any kind of coat you desire—straight, short, wavy, curly. Consult the A.K.C. book for details.

NORWEGIAN ELKHOUND

The real name of the dog is *Grahund* which translated into English is "grey dog." The dog has none of the characteristics of a hound. It is the common farm dog of Norway and a truly grand dog of medium size.

The first were brought in by the Rookwood Kennels of Lexington, Ky. You will find an illustration and description of the breed in their catalogue issued about 1916. It was called Bear Dog then. The second dogs were brought in during the First World War by a New Yorker who was one of the delegates on Henry Ford's Peace Ship. The dogs' owner permitted them to bark unduly, and word went out they were yappers. Actually they are about average in this respect.

The Grahund is to Norway what the farm shepherd is to America, except that it is not as competent a herder. It is used to hunt, but this hunting is done on a chain; the hunter takes advantage of the better olfactory capacity of his dog. The dog smells an elk or a herd and leads the hunter upwind to within shooting range. In all of the European languages except English there is no word for *hound*. All breeds are *Hunde:* Blut-hund (Blood-dog). Those who introduced the Grahund over here called it *Elkhound* and gave the public an entirely errone-ous impression of the breed.

In Sweden, the larger dog of the same type—the Alghund (Moose dog)—is used principally for moose hunting. It is not a hound. It does not necessarily lead his handler to the moose, but rather it finds a moose and barks at it, holding it in one place by keeping the animal's attention so that the hunter can come close enough to shoot. In Sweden there are many moose hunting contests with these fine dogs which look a good deal like Alsatians but have much more dependable temperaments.

I included Alghunden in the classification of breeds because they are one of the more abundant breeds. They certainly will be brought here when the public learns how superior they are to many of the breeds now popular. Will the A.K.C. put them in the class with scent hounds, as they did with the Grahund? Let us hope not.

TERRIERS

American Fox Terrier

In most of the United States the fox terrier is a very short-coated, smallish dog, mostly white with a broad head and a small, pointed nose. The ears are generally like those of bats, or they may tip over at the ends.

When I was a boy, every dog act in vaudeville included these fox terriers. They are so eager to please and so responsive that, like poodles, they have always been favorite trick dogs.

English Fox Terriers

If you have never seen the American breed described above, but have watched the "Thin Man" movies you will think of a fox terrier as a wire-haired, long, narrow-headed breed, full of zip and energy, mostly white, and never possessing bat ears. What you don't know or read about this type is that they are jittery, full of springs, and "born with a chip on their shoulders." They are great barkers, too, but like all fox terriers, they can easily be taught to be quiet vocally, if not physically.

Persons buying them should realize that several times a year the dog must be either plucked or clipped—an expense which can cost as much, or more than, the dog's annual food bill—if he is to be kept in proper condition. The "wire," as he is called, is especially subject to skin disease.

Long-Legged British Terriers

In size the Airedale stands first, the Kerry blue next, and then Irish, Bedlington, Lakeland, Welsh, Norwich, and fox, in approximately this order. There are fox terriers larger than Welsh and Irish larger than small Airedales. But despite this overlapping there *is* a breed size difference. If a terrier is a dog for digging, getting into an animal's burrow or rock pile, one wonders why the "terrier" title has been given to some of the larger breeds in this group. The Airedale is more like an otterhound (a wire-haired true hound) than he is like a Scotty or a Norwich.

They are all unusually courageous. (The otterhound with his courage, wire coat, and toughness could well be included with them.) The breed tends to be spunky, alert, and make excellent watchdogs.

The Kerry blue starts life as a black dog and should become blue as the black hair falls and is replaced by a faded shade. Sometimes he fails to turn. I know one which changed color on his third shed. This is a gamble you take in buying a Kerry blue puppy.

The Bedlington has a coat much like the other terriers, but

softer. It grows more and longer hair on the face than most breeds. If you have only seen the show dog, you wouldn't recognize it before it was barbered. The hair is left quite long on the foreface and on the forehead, and the clipping pattern gives the appearance of a lamb.

In this general group Airedale and fox terriers stand well above the others numerically.

Two generations ago the Airedale was the dog of the hour. The breed was then what the Alsatian (German shepherd) is today. They were everywhere, and they had many uses. Moreover, they were larger than the present-day show Airedale. It is too bad that they dropped in popularity because there is nothing an Alsatian can do that an Airedale can't do as well or better. In addition, Airedales are quite fair natural trailers. For many years the great Indian athlete, Jim Thorp, worked with a special family of these fine dogs—the Oorang Airedales—and helped make them more popular. They were the best police dogs ever used although they had a reputation for killing sheep. I never heard of one killing a human being.

Short-Legged British Terriers

These dogs have similar temperaments but vary in physical appearance. They are intelligent with the terrier courage and the terrier propensity to dig when the opportunity affords. One and all make ideal companions. We have the Cairn, the West Highland white, Scottish, Sealyham, Dandie Dinmont and Skye terriers. With the exception of the Dandie Dinmont they need to be kept plucked or clipped. When the word "clipping" is used, I realize that show fanciers will take issue with me because they say clipping makes the hair come in finer, whereas plucking makes it coarser—the desired type of coat for wirehaired terriers. This is merely an opinion. After having clipped the same wire-haired dogs for six years and compared their coats with those of brothers and sisters that had been plucked when it again came time for grooming and both had their full growth of coats, I could see no difference in the texture. There is a difference, however, in the *appearance* of a clipped and a plucked dog; only the plucked should be considered for showing.

Of these short-legged little dogs, the Scottie is most reserved and the Cairn probably the most demonstrative. Scottie breeders have been plagued by a strain of timidity that has run through the breed—a most unterrier-like characteristic. Breeders are rapidly eliminating this trait.

Breeders in America have used these terriers so little for the work for which they were originally developed that today one would not be able to obtain a puppy with any assurance of its value for true terrier work. For this reason, and since no one cares, the dogs have been developed strictly for pets and small, alert watch dogs. It's rare indeed to encounter one that will bite. One sees a number of these various breeds in the city today, and it is quite possible that they will become much more popular in the future.

Dachshund

The badger dog is in no sense a hound, although it is grouped with hounds in the A.K.C. classifications. The German word *hund* means *dog,* not *hound*. The badger dog is a terrier, bred with short legs to "go to earth" and drive a badger out of its burrow. Years ago the dachshund was quite a large animal. I have seen good typical specimens which weighed seventy pounds, but gradually, over the years the breed has undergone changes, chiefly in size but also in the coat. You may now procure wire-haired or long-haired dachshunds as well as the more common smooth-coated type. The tendency has been toward the toy size, and of the dachshunds that I have seen, the small ones predominate in popularity. Breeders tell me that frequently the first question asked by prospective purchasers is, "Will the puppy be large when grown?" If so, they do not want it.

Dachshunds are clean, neat dogs, tending to be quite odorless, but they have the reputation of being difficult to housebreak, possibly because they can crawl under low furniture to avoid punishment.

The various strains of dachshunds vary in docility. In the case of some show dogs, breeders have given little thought to temperament, with the result that these dogs win prizes in the show ring but not the affection of buyers.

Miniature Schnauzer

The breed is increasing in popularity. Its gray coat is a most practical color. It is wire-haired, so it must be clipped or plucked. It is small in size and full of energy—almost the opposite of the calm cocker spaniel, more on the Boston terrier type, bouncy and considerably more rugged.

The dog's ears are cropped in puppyhood, which give it a pert appearance, especially after grooming. This breed has lots to recommend it. If you have heard that Schnauzers are snappy or ferocious, your informant was probably talking about the giant type of which there are very few in America. There is also a middle size which is a "lot of dog" and excellent as a watchdog.

FIGHTING BREEDS

Only three breeds can honestly be classified as real fighters, that is, bred for the purpose of competing in professional dog fights. Dog fighting, like cock fighting, is still a "sport" in some parts of the world. So far as I know it is illegal all over America, yet there are dozens of dog fights every year, and dogs are still being bred for the purpose. The breeds are bull-terrier, pit bull, and Staffordshire terrier. Pit bulls exceed the others numerically in the U.S.A. Study the ads in *Bloodlines,* the official organ of the U.K.C., and you will see for yourself.

Today the pit bull is more often used as a "catch dog" than for fighting. If you do not know what a catch dog is, you should, because they are common in the South. Wherever hogs are permitted open range (freedom to range without confines) or even in fenced-in areas, it becomes necessary to catch the hogs that have become wild. The herd is located and the desired hog pointed out to the dog. He usually manages to catch hold of the hog's jowl and hold while the owner slips a noose on the animal's hind leg.

Pit bulls are among the most powerful dogs, pound for pound, ever developed and are wonderful human companions.

Staffordshire terriers are much the same but most of those in America today are of a lighter build.

The English bullterrier has been much maligned. Several years ago two incidents occurred in New York City that were extremely regrettable. In the first, a pack of bullterriers was kept on a barge in New York harbor and given very little exercise. Being made, as my father used to say, of rawhide and piano wire, it was no kindness to confine them in such small quarters. Somehow they broke loose and attacked a boy, who either had let them out or just happened to be nearby. A policeman saw the melee, went to the boy's defense, and the dogs charged him and threw him down. A second policeman came to his rescue and shot some of the dogs, as I remember.

The second incident concerned a man who was found floating in the river near the barge, badly lacerated. There was suspicion that the man may have attempted to board the barge and was attacked by the dogs. This was never confirmed.

The publicity given to these pathetic events was so widespread that it did tremendous damage to bullterriers. I recall a beauty which was brought to me to be destroyed, simply because it was a brother of one of the dogs on the barge.

If I know anything about dogs, I know that no greater injustice was ever done a wonderful breed of dog than was committed, not by the dogs, but by the dogs' owner who lived with them on that barge.

Many persons have been killed by dogs. A pair of Great Danes in New Jersey killed a boy who ran along the other side of a fence. Children on bicycles have been bitten so badly by dogs which chased them, that they died. Alsatians (German shepherds) left to guard little babies have pulled them from their cribs and carriages and actually eaten parts of them—something even a wolf will not do. In December 1967 three Alsatians killed two small boys who often played with them. But these far more horrible dog crimes have not been held against these breeds, judging from their continued popularity. Under the same confined conditions, a pack of boxers or greyhounds might have proved equally vicious.

I have owned and handled a considerable number of bullterriers and I have never known one that could not be trusted with humans. No fancier of the breed advises permitting the dogs to run loose. They are a fighting breed—tough, feeling pain less than most—and they seem almost lacking in the sense of self-preservation. Their jaws are extremely powerful. Chasing something alive, catching and killing it, gives them a thrill. Cats are not safe, nor are dogs, in any neighborhood with a bullterrier which has a careless owner. Yet, for all this love of battling, the dog is still ideal around the home. Just don't let him out by himself. If you want a bullterrier you can turn loose, buy a bitch and have her spayed. Don't overfeed her. Unless I'm very much mistaken, you'll find her easy to train, eager to please you, and the short-haired dog of your dreams.

SHEPHERD DOGS

Collie

One of the most superior dogs ever bred is the Scotch collie. Magnificent in its natural state, kind in expression, and with everything in temperament that one could desire—this was the collie of a generation ago when Albert Payson Terhune immortalized the breed with his delightful stories about his Sunnybank dogs. Since that day too many collies have appeared in degenerated form with both physical and mental defects, but it is still possible to find collies with all the true herding attributes. A group of fanciers in the Middlewest have determined to breed the collie in America into the real stock dog it once was the world over and to regain the prominence in the field which has been captured by the American farm shepherd and the border collie.

So many collies have been bred for showing and selected for longer and longer heads that one frequently hears people say that "collies look like anteaters." We also hear them remark that the back of the head has become so small that there is little room for brains. This remark seems logical, but in a study of brain cases at Yale University we found it is untrue. The brain case of an especially narrow-headed collie proved to be equal in size to that of a wide-headed bulldog. If you don't object to a long-haired dog and a high-toned voice it will be difficult for you to find a more satisfactory companion than a fine collie, and this especially applies to anyone wanting a dependable family dog.

American Shepherd

Back in the colonial days, the settlers brought with them many fine dogs, most of them of the collie or shepherd type. Some refuse to call these dogs a breed, yet they have been, as a type, the American dog. As shepherd dogs, they are not quite the equal of the marvelous border collie because the latter is the product of the most stringent selection for sheep herding without too much consideration of temperament. The border collies live away from human habitation much of the time and have not been bred for general farm use.

But the American dog has been a constant human companion as well as the farm shepherd and guard dog. Many have been used as hunters. In an illuminating article in *Field and Stream*, B. B. Titus describes how he used to train these general purpose dogs to hunt raccoons at night and squirrels in the day as well as to herd cows. Many of the dogs were real shepherds.

If you travel anywhere in the U.S.A. you will find, when you get away from the cities, so many more shepherds than any other breed. You'll wonder why they aren't registered in the A.K.C. Can you imagine what would have happened if as many of these dogs were observed by Americans traveling, let us say, in Argentina? Why they would have "given it a breed" long ago, formed a great club, and imported them by the thousand.

We've got the story, the breed—a marvelous breed it is—and we have the uses for it. In ability, it stood at the top of American war dogs. It is one of the few breeds bred for general intelligence. No exaggeration is needed.

This is the dog that can be trusted to guard children day or night. He will bark when the horse has colic or one of the cows calves. He can herd the cows home, let his master know if one is missing, and with some power hard to explain, even force a ewe whose lamb has died to adopt an orphan. He is often the farm boy's hunting companion, and when "Old Shep" passes on, the family often holds a funeral. You'll find many a wooden slab in a field near the farmhouse with "Old Shep" scrawled on it, and you'll know his family was all choked up at the loss.

Yet, while a so-called sheep-herding dog named the Komondor from Hungary is registered in the A.K.C. the American shepherd hasn't even an official breed name.

Corgi

Wales has produced a few breeds, but the Corgi, even with its nondescript shape, should make the Welsh people proud. It is a shepherd dog—short-legged, tough, able to withstand cold winters and outdoor weather, yet so adaptable that it makes an ideal house pet.

Because of its shepherd ancestry, it obeys well with little education, it is a top-flight, keen watchdog and yet of the soundest temperament. The Corgi makes a wonderful family dog. Perhaps you object to the low carriage; you won't if you ever own one because it is really a practically-shaped dog. There are two types, the Cardigan and Pembroke; the latter has a bobbed tail, the former is uncut. The short-tailed type is increasing, and the number of the long-tailed decreasing— there are very few of them in America.

GUARD DOGS

Alsatian Wolfdog (German Shepherd)

Because this breed was developed as an attack dog according to the writings of Von Stephanitz, its real founder, the males need very strict training. My observation of the breed convinces me that not one in every ten males receives this kind of handling, and these dogs grow up without knowing that the owner is the master. Until the males reach maturity at two years they are generally manageable, but at this time they usually can decide who's boss.

Of course, as everyone knows, there is now much timidity among both males and females. This is the result of poor breeding. For a long time complimentary publicity in movies, television, and in the press, made any German shepherd easy to sell. The biggest boost was from those awful early Rin Tin Tin and Strongheart movies. But the public loved it. And they were determined to acquire one of these dogs which would do their thinking for them!

Then came the "Seeing Eye" movement. Now I know that it is a most unpopular statement to make, but although Seeing Eye is an admirable institution, in the beginning they used the wrong kind of dogs. I tried in vain, in those early days, to encourage them to use other breeds but the organizers were chiefly German Police Dog breeders. I was a lone voice. Since then many of those interested have told me how right I was.

In England and Germany the breed is called the Alsatian wolfdog. It started off in America as the German police dog, but the name was soon realized to be detrimental to sales. It rang of severity, and its connotation was generally bad. So the fanciers induced the A.K.C. to permit a change of the name to something the breed is not—a shepherd dog. The registrations in the A.K.C. zoomed to fifteen hundred a month—before the public caught on to the fact that families are not police agents. They bought the dogs. A tremendous advertising campaign had been responsible for the increase, and the buyer just didn't realize what he was getting.

So it was not surprising, when the reaction set in, that A.K.C. registrations dropped from fifteen hundred a month down to sixty-seven. Those who still fancied the breed realized something must be done. The Seeing Eye started the breed on the upgrade again, but the public was not told that the trainers and owners found spayed females were the most trustworthy, reliable and tractable. The males again went to the general public.

When the war came, the German shepherd was chosen as a war dog. We acted at the Whitney Veterinary Clinic using it as a sort of reception center. German shepherds were brought and kept until we received word to ship them. The owners were supposedly giving their dogs for patriotic reasons. The truth is that we didn't handle a single one whose owner wasn't happy to be rid of an untrustworthy pet. Some we had to handle with a pipe and loop of wire on the end to avoid being attacked. I often wondered how much conditioning it took to make those animals useful.

Fanciers excuse their vicious dogs by calling them fear-biters. They go skulking off into a corner, and when you go near, they urinate and snap at you. From my studies in dog psychology, I know that a lot of this is merely bad training, and many of these fear-biters can be completely cured and made into fairly bold, unafraid dogs. But don't you agree that it would be better to breed sounder basic temperaments which do not need extra training?

German shepherds are still the Army dog, but the handlers now take the time to choose those purchased more carefully. Had they decided on a breed such as our inexpensive American farm shepherds, selection of the right individuals would have been easier.

A basic fault in the German shepherd is its propensity to kill small dogs. Dogs of its own size are avoided, but I have had to suture altogether too many mangled little dogs which German shepherds have attacked.

Ask any delivery clerk which dogs he fears most. I ask every time I have a chance. This is the standard reply: Dobermans, German shepherds, and some mongrels, with these breeds predominating in that order.

But there's a good side to the German shepherd. Now and then a really nice trustworthy animal appears. I have known many of them but generally these are not used as breeders. And they are the very ones which should be! If care were used, I'm sure we could breed, within three dog generations, a strain of German shepherd that would be everything the fanciers of the breed claimed in their early exaggerations.

There are few more striking looking breeds, alert breeds, or breeds whose attention is more easily kept. They should now be bred for a temperament as admirable as their appearance.

Doberman Pinscher

A male Doberman is a lot of dog—much too much for the average owner. Everything about the dog is *sharp* from his bark to his actions. He emits more barks per minute than any dog of any other breed with which I am acquainted. When he looks at someone he doesn't like, through the bars of a cage or when on a chain—with his curled-up lip, drawn-up nose, and flashing white fangs—he is the picture of the ferocious guard dog.

I have never known a person who was acquainted with other breeds of fine dogs to buy a Doberman for a pet; always they are persons who start with the breed and, having nothing with which to compare them, continue in the fancy. Several I've known continued until so many of the pups they had sold matured into ferocious individuals that they had to concede they had erred.

But if you are old enough to remember the publicity campaign that was used to introduce the breed, you will realize how difficult it was to resist the temptation to jump into the fancy.

As in the case of "German shepherds," the males take a lot

of severe handling to be controllable. They are almost ideal dogs for guard duty—when it does little harm if an intruder is badly bitten. In Macy's store they are used as companions to the watchmen. Good! And it's great publicity for Macy's too. This is the place for the males, and there are many such jobs.

But don't be misled by the claims of man-training ability; their olfactory ability is low. Many hunters tried them on game, but they could only smell very fresh tracks. Again, as in the case of German shepherds, females spayed when about five to six months of age make wonderful pets; but they have a tendency to become uncommonly overweight. They also tend to develop fatty tumors—more so than dogs of any other breed, if my figures are representative. And I believe they are.

I often wonder whatever became of the all-red Doberman? At the time of their introduction one would see many all-red dogs with black noses and dark eyes—much more handsome than the liver-and-tan "red" ones with their yellow eyes. Somewhere real reds were lost, and this is unfortunate.

In America there are a few docile strains whose males and females are equally tractable, but Dobermans are mainly show specimens. One expensive dog toured the country and won best-in-show many times, but even his handler dared not cross him. Every judge who passed on him was warned not to touch him. I saw him lunge at a judge when he was receiving his award. Had I been the judge I would have said, "Take this dog out and never bring a beast like that into another show ring or I'll see that your license as a handler is revoked." He didn't; he gave this dog best-in-show, and that vicious temperament was passed on to probably hundreds of puppies. He *was* a good-looking dog, and that particular judge rationalized by remarking, "He's a guard dog; that's what he was bred to be. He was simply protecting his handler." Well, if you need that kind of dog, buy a Doberman.

Boxer

The breed began its rapid rise just a short time ago, quickly reached its peak, and is now somewhat less popular. Good ones, with their cropped ears and tails, present a snappy appearance, especially the tan dogs with white socks. In addition there are homely, dark brindles which few persons seem to want and many whites with tan spots illegally registered as tan-and-white. These are often used in breeding. In the makeup of the breed, white dogs are obviously used because of the large number of white pups still appearing in litters of solid-colored dogs.

The boxer is a guard dog and nothing else. Some call it a "meat burner" because it is so useless for hunting, sheepherding or any other such work. Boxers are easy to keep as pets, although they have a tendency to become fat. Most of them become phlegmatic as they age, and few seem to live past twelve. One sees many puffy, slow, lethargic boxers, especially in cities.

It is a breed which, to be at its best, needs room to run. And in the country boxers can present problems because they are livestock killers. Those who have had greatest satisfaction with the breed keep only one and keep it well controlled. Many persons object to the snorting, but this can be corrected surgically by veterinarians. On the whole, it isn't comparable to many of our American breeds of the same size—breeds kept natural and which need no surgery to make them presentable or satisfactory.

The boxer is practically a sprightly (when young) undershot, small edition of the ponderous mastiff, trimmed to be stylish. The bull-mastiff was started in England as a new breed at the same time as the boxer was started in Germany. The two developed along slightly different lines. The bull-mastiff is much the same kind of dog but uncropped.

Schipperke

I have always wondered why Schipperkes (little skippers) are not more popular. For those who like a spry, alert dog with a practical coat and extremely rugged constitution, well, where can they find anything better? It is a Belgian dog, probably with herding ancestry, but used on barges. The temperaments are almost always sound, the dog responds to training with ease, and it is an excellent watch dog.

The color is black, and there is no tail; some are bob-tailed, and some must be docked to be in style. Perhaps the movies or television will take one up someday—then watch this wonderful little breed achieve the popularity it deserves.

Chow Chow

The chow chow is known the world over as the dog with the black tongue. This fluffy, thick, and soft-coated breed which we see in cream, red, black, and blue colors is genuinely one of the oldest known breeds. It was popularized like several others as the great all-purpose dog. We were told it was the best bird dog, the best hound dog, the best guard dog, the best everything. We were not told that the males especially were sullen, and aloof, and quite unpredictable. The breed's popularity, some years back, was accounted for by the false advertising and the almost irresistible charm of the litttle puppies. Talk about the "puppy in the pet-shop window"! Gradually after many people had been bitten by males, the great fad for the breed diminished. The few breeders who were left determined to select for better dispositions. They found that spayed females made dependable and attractive companions, although they were somewhat phlegmatic. They also learned from the hunters who had tried them that compared to the American breeds they were virtually worthless, and they no longer advertised their dogs for these purposes.

Proponents claim, with some truth, that the breed is easily housebroken—but the claim we formerly heard that chows never have fleas is of course untrue. Chows are particularly prone to skin disease and most especially to the type known as "weeping eczema."

I personally think the chow has been done a great injustice, and I base this opinion on my conversations with Chinese hunters who have told me that the specimens that were taken to England and thence to America were not in the least representative of the hunting dogs of China. In the first place, there are no chow chows, by that name, in China. There *are* dogs of a similar type which make most efficient hunting dogs, but these were not brought to America. Those we know were chiefly kept for guard dogs and came from the Canton Province.

Bulldog

Most persons call it the "English bulldog" but *bulldog* is its name. As the bloodhound is a symbol of determination and staying power, the bulldog is the symbol of grit and tenacity, often being pictured along with John Bull, the symbolic Englishman. Bulldogs are quite placid but playful. Their value as watchdogs is their reputation. Once aroused a bulldog can be a formidable antagonist, and his crushing bite is powerful. I saw one break the front leg of a large dog with one bite. He likes to hang on when he takes hold, not fight slashingly.

The loud snoring is objectionable to many, and their liability to heat strokes makes it necessary to watch them in summer and provide shade.

I find that many admirers have a false idea of what a good specimen should look like, and it is easy to sell poor quality dogs to the public. The ideal does not call for tremendously wide chests with the legs appearing to be stuck on the sides. Such dogs break down quickly. Study the standard before you buy; you may be surprised.

SLED DOG BREEDS

These are powerful dogs, medium to large in size, with extremely thick coats. They are closer to the wolf than other breeds, and many sled dog teams are three-quarters wolf. Developed by men for hard work and even dispositions, it is natural that they make fine companions in northern areas. In the South some persons claim that the dogs tend to suffer from skin diseases. They probably like to howl more than dogs of other breeds.

The malamute and the Siberian husky are the principal breeds. The Eskimo dog is often spoken of, but it is rare. The Samoyed is quite popular, tending to replace the chow in popularity because of its more dependable disposition.

The Samoyed is all white, but not an albino. The name means *cannibal* in Russian, and some say the breed came from a tribe which once were actually cannibals.

At one time the spitz—like a small Samoyed in appearance, but coming in many colors—was a very popular dog in America. It was of Finnish origin. For years it was eclipsed but now is increasing again in popularity. Unfortunately, a so-called spitz is too often a long-haired twenty- to thirty-pound mongrel. It is one of the older breeds and is registered by the U.K.C.

The true sled dogs registered by the A.K.C. are now bred for show and racing, since helicopters and planes handle their previous work.

GIANT DOGS

Great Dane

This German giant, for all its size and apparent power, is frequently referred to by those who know dogs as the "violet" among the breeds. While it is true that there are a few strains that are still used for hunting, notably in Australia, this breed, which was once the boar hound, has pretty much lost its vital characteristics and has become a beautiful showpiece. There are few more majestic animals in appearance, whether their ears are cropped or uncropped.

The Dane seems to need a placid, even existence in order to maintain its weight and appearance. As any boarding kennel owner will tell you, most Danes can be expected to lose twenty pounds within a week or two in unfamiliar surroundings. Apparently they become frightfully homesick.

Danes have been bred in striking colors ranging from fawn to black to harlequin, which is white with black splotches. In the matter of voice, the Dane is an exception to the other German breeds; his voice is deep, not harsh and not particularly voluminous—hardly in keeping with the size of the dog. But many a Dane left at home alone or boarded in a kennel will just stand for hours and bark.

The Great Dane is probably the shortest lived of all the breeds. Seldom does one pass nine years in anything that approaches sound health.

Giant Long-Haired Breeds

St. Bernards, Newfoundlands, and Great Pyrenees offer an opportunity for selection for those who want a lumbering long-haired giant. The "Saint" also comes in a short-haired model. It is sable or sable-and-white; the Newfoundland is black and also black-and-white, à la the Landseer pattern; the

Great Pyrenees is all white. Of the three the Great Pyrenees is the most agile and least clumsy.

The Newfoundland is the world's greatest water dog; it loves water, is attracted to it, and is even able to dive like a seal and swim below the surface. This fact must be taken into consideration if you live near water. If you want a dog easily trained in life saving, the Newfoundland is *the* dog; if you especially do *not* want a dog that loves to get wet, it is the breed to avoid. For personality, the Newfoundland is one of the grandest dogs to own.

My experience with St. Bernards causes me to warn that the dogs of this breed are not all saints by any means. I've seen many degenerates with naturally miserable temperaments. I've also seen many with defective hindquarters due to heredity, not diet. If you buy one, demand a pup from truly representative parents.

Great Pyrenees dogs tend to become smaller without drastic selection. Be sure you buy yours from a litter whose parents and near kin are typical of giants. If you get one which turns out be too small, your friends will refuse to recognize it as a real purebred.

Recent research indicates that underfeeding during the growth period produces somewhat smaller dogs than does adequate feeding. Give your giant puppy all it can eat throughout its growing period because size is important in all of these breeds.

TOY DOGS

Pekingese

The Pekingese is a long-haired, short-legged Chinese dog with a foreshortened face and with courage out of all proportion to its size. The breed is growing rapidly in popularity for the dogs make almost ideal house pets. The A.K.C. figures do not tell the whole story because a large number of these dogs are also registered in the U.K.C. Of the Pekes I have seen, there has been little difference between the U.K.C. and the A.K.C., although one would expect a greater perfection with reference to showing in the A.K.C. because of the many dog shows in which Pekes are judged.

Fortunately, large dogs seldom condescend to fight so small an object as a Pekingese or a lot of them would be killed, because male Pekes will attack dogs of any size. The big dog seldom fights back, unless it is an Alsatian, in which case the Peke will usually be mangled or killed.

Probably the greatest hazard in buying one of these dogs, with its retroussé face, is the danger of its becoming blind early in life, for no breed is more bug-eyed. It has been bred so that its huge eyes are especially prominent, and they protrude so that there is no bony or fleshy protection. Moreover, between the nose and eyes, a roll of skin stands up. The hair growing on this skin in many cases actually rubs against the eyes and must be kept clipped short, or the eye cornea may become so badly irritated that it will become opaque. Not being able to see out of one eye, the dog bumps into objects on that side and injures the eye still more until eventually it must be removed. One sees more one-eyed Pekes than dogs of any other breed.

Pomeranian

A sort of midget sled dog, the Pom looks like an animated thistle—with its hair tending to stand out straight from its body and with an abundant under coat. A good Pom seldom weighs over seven pounds. It comes in several colors from black to cream. Its ears are erect, its eyes are quite far apart, and its nose is medium in length and not sharp.

Poms are extremely alert and, if encouraged, become incessant barkers, which makes them wonderful watchdogs even though their diminutive size would hardly frighten an intruder.

The coat needs some combing and brushing, and the dog must be watched for skin diseases, especially in hot climates. The coat is really so warm and protective that these little dogs can be kept in unheated kennels in the North and still thrive. Despite their appearance, there is probably no more rugged or longer-lived dog among all the toy breeds.

Chihuahua

In response to the desire on the part of thousands for a small, short-haired, trouble-free pooch, Chihuahua breeders have produced many puppies, but these are not nearly enough to supply the demand and hence the high prices.

Chihuahuas are delicate in the tiny midget sizes, but quite rugged little dogs in the upper reaches of their permissible size. Too, they are amazingly long-lived when properly fed. But how many owners do feed them properly? Because these dogs are small and constantly close at hand, it is a great temptation to feed them what they want, not what is best for them. And to feed a three-pound dog, very little food is required. In terms of butter, two chips would have sufficient calories, if not many of the other dietary essentials.

A great deal of nonsense has been written about this so-called "native dog of Mexico." There never was any native dog of Mexico. The only dogs the Spaniards found were probably prairie dogs. The real Chihuahua must have been brought in with the Spaniards on their ships but from where no one knows. China, perhaps. Even so, for all this uncertainty about their origin, the dogs *were* introduced to us from Mexico and have been kept true midgets by selection. There is so great a resemblance between the smallest American fox terriers and the Chihuahuas that there can be no doubt that considerable undercover crossing has occurred. American fox terriers are often sold as Chihuahuas and larger Chihuahuas are sold as American fox terriers.

Two reasons for the high prices of these midgets are the smallness of the litters and the more and more frequent need for Caesarean operations. When a bitch has one or two pups per litter, and the operation costs from twenty to fifty dollars, the pups cannot be sold cheaply. Breeders frequently keep quite a number of bitches because the cost of maintenance is low, a dozen costing little more to feed than one German shepherd bitch, and the dozen produce more pups in the aggregate than the one large bitch. Even so, as Tom Paine said, " 'Tis dearness which gives everything its value," so with the breed's fanciers increasing so rapidly and the supply short, we may see a rapid deterioration. Already hundreds are being sold that are quite untypical of the breed standard. How many are midget American fox terriers it is hard to say, but I have seen many that made me suspicious. If you buy one, memorize the standard, look at some good ones and be sure the pup matches that image. The true Chihuahua is easy to handle, easy to train, and costs little or nothing to feed—a nice diminutive dog. But watch out for an exaggerated "apple head." The big skull may indicate hydrocephalus ("water on the brain"). Altogether too many Chihuahuas suffer from this defect.

Toy Manchester

This tiny model of the standard Manchester used to be bred very small, but they may now be as heavy as twelve pounds and still be considered of proper size. There are probably more registered in the U.K.C. than in the A.K.C. But you'll find good ones with papers from either club.

The short hair, tiny voice, affectionate temperament, robust constitution, and the general ease of caring account for their rapid increase in popularity. Those wanting black or very dark dogs choose a toy Manchester, those wanting a light or white-colored dog choose a Chihuahua or a toy American fox terrier.

UNCLASSIFIED BREEDS

Poodle

Everyone knows what a poodle looks like, but few persons know how the dog appears before it is clipped. It is definitely a luxury pet and one of the most expensive dogs to maintain whether it be the standard, miniature, or toy. Many persons, however, have learned to do their own clipping and grooming, in which case this consideration does not apply.

The poodle was at one time a French and German general-purpose dog. There is still considerable innate retrieving behavior in the make-up of the large poodles, and we are told that it was once used for bird hunting in France. In the field, the dogs are used with their coats clipped short and resemble hounds. Don't let anyone tell you that the standard poodle is a sissy dog. They only look that way in their fancy clips. They are dogs of great character and individuality. It has been aptly said that they are the only dogs that are born ladies and gentlemen. I wouldn't agree with the "only," but they are very well mannered.

All three types are quick to learn and exceedingly responsive. It is unfortunate that with such wonderful natural material more of them are not properly trained to exhibit their potential intelligence and usefulness. Too many are kept simply as ornaments to have around the house.

Poodle colors are most attractive. You can find almost any color to suit your taste, and sometimes these dogs are even tinted with harmless vegetable dyes. Your pet can be made to match your car or your costume.

The latest innovation is the dog spotted with white which is now permitted registration by the A.K.C.

Pug

It so happens that my grandparents almost always had a pair of pugs. Naturally, having seen what wonderfully satisfactory dogs they were, I've kept a warm spot in my heart for the breed ever since. It is good to see the breed climbing back into well-deserved popularity.

There's only one detrimental feature in a pug to watch for—his eyes. What I have to say about Pekingese applies here. Both breeds, because of their large, prominent eyes, frequently injure them and develop ulcers. Even when healed the scar is disfiguring.

Of all the small dogs pugs probably need Caesarean operation less frequently than any other breed, and they are uncommonly prolific. It is not unusual for one of these little dogs to whelp and raise eight puppies. Their color is a practical gray or a black. The hair is thick but short, and the temperaments of all I have known were placid and perhaps a little reserved. Compared with a fidgety Boston, a pug is almost phlegmatic, but ready to go and appreciative of attention.

Boston Terrier

Here is a little American dog that started out as a sound, small dog, but has rapidly been bred into a bundle of nerves, much tinier in size than the originators envisioned. For those who do not mind a jumpy, fidgety animal, the Boston terrier can be good demonstrative pet. Its short hair is easily kept and of a practical color.

The breed's chief drawback is the frequent need for Caesarean operations due to show standards which demand a large head and front-end tapering to an unusually small hind-end. To those who are not interested in breeding, this is of no concern. Bostons need extra attention in extremely hot weather due to their constricted throats, and many have delicate digestive systems with a frequent tendency to vomit after eating. Bostons can now be obtained that are practically midgets, with accompanying midget voices. My observations indicate that the smaller types tend to be more nervous than the larger types. Some of the old-fashioned larger Bostons made excellent house pets, and there are still some available today.

Dalmatian

This coach dog, which was evolved to run behind the heels of a horse or between the front wheels of a horse-drawn vehicle, is still a natural companion to horses. The breed has long been a trademark for fire engine companies, and they sometimes still keep Dalmatians for mascots. With their black spots and gleaming white coats, they immediately catch the eye.

Today the Dalmatian is kept almost exclusively as a guard dog and has few other uses. Many dog experts remark that the breed is a prize example of emotional deterioration. My own experience with them indicates that although there are still many with sound temperaments available, there are altogether too many jittery fear-biters being sold. My early impression of them, and I knew a great many even as a boy, was of a stolid but alert, responsive, and easily trained animal. In almost every circus, a Dalmatian and horse act was featured. Horse men have long held the opinion that there is something in a Dalmatian's make-up that pacifies horses. This may be because the coach dog was so carefully selected for this purpose.

Considerable research has been attempted with Dalmatians.

One discovery was that even the distance they trotted behind a horse's heels was inherited. Other research showed that the Dalmatian color is apparently associated with an abnormality in the urine, which does not, however, seem to shorten the dog's life. There is considerable deafness in the breed.

Should you buy a Dalmatian puppy, don't expect that its markings will be the same when grown; the puppies are born white. This is one of the gambles that you take. You may get a foul-marked dog or a champion. For this reason it is better, when possible, to buy an older puppy whose spots have become distinct.

Basenji

Also called the "barkless dog," the Basenji has a character of its own as well as a unique appearance. It is tan, of medium size and has a short coat. It is not sculptured nor does it need barbering. It is a natural dog and a clean, easily-cared-for animal.

Owners say it is affectionate. It is very quick and is used for hunting in its native country, but hunting of a special kind and in packs. The few sounds it emits would not make it attractive to American hunters, and so it seems destined here to be strictly a pet.

Mongrel

Because mongrels are so numerous, no dog book would be complete without some discussion of their virtues and drawbacks. Over the years the word "cur" has often been applied to a mongrel. As though the two were synonymous! My dictionary defines a cur as a "snarling, worthless, or outcast dog." A cur is not necessarily a mixed breed, obviously, but the word has so often been applied to mongrels that it has become a word of disparagement commonly used in speaking of them.

Some, in fact many, mongrels are tops as dogs. The trouble with the majority is that they are not specialists; they're just potentially fine dogs, and that tells it all. Their excellence stems from the unusual vigor that hybridizing often engenders. They combine the dominant characteristics of both parents. Sometimes these dominant characteristics are good and sometimes harmful.

Much as I have admired some mongrels, I can think of few ways in which a mongrel is as valuable or useful as a purebred. They often make good watchdogs, but are they any better than either of their purebred parents?

They are inferior sires and dams because their offspring are unpredictable. They cannot be registered, and because they usually have no specific use, they have low commercial value. Generally, mongrels are given away. In puppy kennels they may be bought for from two to ten dollars each.

There are breeds that are similar except for color. The setters come to mind. Crosses of Gordon with English technically make mongrels which may not be registered, but *are* they mongrels? Crosses of bluetick coonhounds with Redbones are technically mongrels, but the offspring are excellent as coondogs and all red in color. They cannot be registered, but they are not really mongrels. When I say *mongrel* I mean a dog resulting from a cross from dogs representing breeds developed for different purposes or, if for the same purpose, of considerable difference in appearance.

While the mongrel is usually not adept at any specific job, there are crosses which are exceedingly useful. Dog owners in England seem loath to discuss the dogs that meant more to the British army during the war than any other kind—*lurchers*.

Lurchers are highly trainable and intelligent dogs produced

by crossing breeds with low tail carriage—Scottish deerhounds with bullterriers and collies with greyhounds, for example. There are very few of them around today, but the real lurchers were trained to be thieves, to catch and kill rabbits on English estates, and to carry them to their owners, who waited on nearby roads. They were trained to steal in various other ways too. But, came the war, and they were all conscripted. They made superb sentries and messengers.

Many sledge dogs are mongrels, some being half or three-quarters wolf. Hybrid vigor helps such dogs but it is questionable whether mongrels are as dependable as the breeds evolved for the purpose—dogs such as Siberian huskies or Alaskan malamutes. To give the devil his due, however, I suppose we must acknowledge that every breed originally had a mongrel heritage. Even today, some breeds give away the secret of their mongrel origins by producing puppies that are recessives. Some call them "throwbacks." Irish setters now and then have black-and-tan puppies; boxers, as we saw, often produce white or almost all-white puppies; Weimaraners produce black and sometimes long-haired pups; and Airedales can produce smooth-haired, houndy looking pups. Black-and-tan and Redbone hounds produce tricolored, buckskin, or liver-and-tan colored pups. Pointers rarely produce long-haired offspring, but German shepherd pups often appear with long, woolly hair. Wire-haired fox terriers have smooth-coated pups —and so it goes. There are those who may say that these facts indicate a recent mismating, but that need not be so at all. It indicates that these breeds still carry the genes of one of the ancestors used in creating the breed. When both sire and dam possess these long-hidden chromosomes, the pairing can give rise to offspring that proclaim the mongrel ancestry.

No, we can't simply say "mongrels are no good," but we must admit that generally they have no advantages over the purebred and realize they are unpredictable as puppies. Fortunately, I made a recent discovery that will prevent the birth of unwanted mongrels. If you own a purebred bitch that manages to mate, and you don't wish the pups, your veterinarian can inject it any time during the first six weeks of pregnancy with a drug, called Malucidin, made from brewery waste, which will end the pregnancy, but not cause an abortion. The fetuses appear to turn into lumps of red jelly and in a few days liquefy and disappear.

Chapter Four

YOUR NEW DOG IN THE HOME

PREPARING FOR THE DOG

Assuming that you have made up your mind and chosen your companion-to-be for, you hope, twelve or more years, what next? How shall you get him home? And are you prepared at home to receive him? Let's get prepared first.

Your decision as to what sort of dog your puppy is to be determines this preparation. House dog or outdoor dog? Let's begin by considering the house dog, since most American dogs are house dogs. In that case there is no need to ask where he has previously been kept; he can be brought directly into your home—no acclimatization is necessary.

THE INDOOR PUPPY

Prepare a small pen for the pup, the size of which will depend on *his* size. For example, make it three feet square for a beagle or cocker pup, four feet square for a collie or boxer. Put a small box in it for his bed, or use a prepared bed. He will learn to sleep in the bed and not to defecate on the pillow or whatever is used for his mattress—a piece of carpet, perhaps, or some old soft rags. Put flat newspaper on the floor so his puppy feet may become accustomed to the feel of it. This is important in housebreaking, as you will see in Chapter Seven.

Some people prefer to use an entire room rather than a pen. Most often the kitchen is used for the pup, and papers are spread over the floor. This is not nearly so sensible a procedure as building a small pen. The pen can be made of a wood frame with chicken wire stapled to the sides of the woodwork. Or it can be a large flat packing case with the top removed. Light plywood packing cases are very suitable and can usually be obtained from a neighborhood electrical appliance store where they have been removed from ranges, refrigerators, radios, and so forth.

There are a number of manufacturers who make indoor pens with hatches attached. One company makes a collapsible wire pen which can be folded and taken in a car or stood on end, folded, in the closet when it is not in use.

Beds

Dog beds can be bought at any pet store. Get a metal frame bed with a tough canvas mattress. Do not get a wickerware bed. It offers an enticement to chew, and most such beds are chewed to bits before a puppy is half grown. Also, many a puppy has had the material stick in his throat or stomach, necessitating a trip to the veterinarian.

THE OUTDOOR PUPPY

Indoor dogs are often kept outdoors in back yards part of their lives. Preparations for these puppies or for those to be kept as watchdogs, or for hunters or dogs which for one reason or another must be kept out of doors all their lives, must be quite different.

Research shows that if the pup is brought up in an outdoor kennel and has plenty of bedding under him, he tolerates low temperatures very well. But no dog, even the short-haired dog, can tolerate being kept in a warm temperature most of the time and then being put out during cold hours.

In winter it is surprising how much cold he can stand. Your pup may persist in tearing the cloth off the door and come bouncing out in the morning in apparent perfect comfort. If there is not an abundance of bedding, especially under the pup, he may not freeze, but he will be most uncomfortable. On extremely cold nights the outdoor puppy may be brought into a somewhat warmer place, such as an unheated cellar or a vestibule, but never into the warm house.

Size of house

What is the proper size for the doghouse? One sees small cocker pups put out in the winter into expensive doghouses built for Saint Bernards. This is cruel, because the puppy has too much house to heat with his small body. The puppy's house should be as small as he can get into comfortably. There should be enough bedding so that he can make a nest for himself. Straw is excellent for this purpose. A perfect kennel for a puppy can be made from a small keg or barrel with a hole in the front. Have it rest on four stones or posts driven part way into the ground so that it cannot roll. As the puppy grows, a larger barrel can be substituted. If you already have a large doghouse, put the barrel or box inside it.

In summer the size of the house makes little difference. On hot nights the pup won't go into his small house, preferring to lie outside where it is cooler.

Kenneling

As a puppy grows he may be chained to his house, to a wire, or kept in a pen. This applies to the dog kept outdoors all his life, to the dog kept outside and brought in occasionally, or to the indoor dog put outside occasionally.

First, the chain. If you attach a chain to a doghouse, the distance from the house to the end of the chain represents the total distance your pup can travel. If you buy a stake with a swivel in the top and drive it into the ground a distance from the house the same length chain allows the pup more freedom, and he does not get his chain twisted around the house and cry for you to come out and free him.

A puppy kept on a chain that drags the ground needs careful attention to be sure he is free from worms. The chain spreads his stools and makes it much more difficult to pick them up.

The chain attached to a pulley or ring that slides along a taut overhead wire is a favorite fastening or tying-out method of many experienced persons. House dogs are frequently "given their exercise" that way. Thousands of dog owners take Fido to the back door, attach the other end of the chain to the dog's collar, and let the dog go. Some of the overhead wires may run fifty or more feet to a tree or to the back fence.

For young, small-type puppies this method is not desirable, but three-month-old pups of large breeds may be kept satisfactorily on chains attached to wires.

Other dog owners have houses in the yard and leave the dogs out all day, knowing that in case of rain the dogs can go into the house.

Wire enclosures

A simple enclosure of woven wire may best serve your purpose as a daytime kennel or an all-year-round one. The quality, strength, and height of the wire will depend on your breed of dog. For short-legged breeds, four-foot-high wire is sufficient. Most breeds will stay inside of a five-foot-high enclosure. Large, agile breeds, such as hounds, pointers, Doberman pinschers, and German shepherds, will need a six-foot-high fence. If your dog jumps that, then all you need do is put wire across the top. The most satisfactory fencing I have found for a reasonable price is the type made and sold under many trade names, such as Acme and Climax.

Second best is fox-farm netting, a hexagonal mesh of heavy gauge. Page or link fencing is excellent but more expensive.

Any woven wire used around your puppy pen, which all too soon becomes a dog pen, should be sunk eight inches into the ground. Better still is a cement slab or curbing that goes deep enough to be beneath the frost line and eight inches to a foot above the ground. The lower edge of the wire mesh then rests on top of the slab.

You may prefer to buy ready-made fences manufactured by one of the companies which advertise in dog magazines. These are excellent, neat and with doors and latches which are dogproof.

Mistakes to avoid in kenneling

There are a number of mistakes that people make when providing a place for their puppies to live. Some will put a bed in the cellar and just let the puppy use the floor. The odor soon fills the house, and the concrete pores of the cellar floor afford an excellent repository for worm eggs. Another mistake is to put the pup so far away from the house that he can't be heard.

He then usually doesn't get the care he needs—"out of sight, out of mind."

Every dog needs a shady spot during the day. He may even dig a hole in the ground to get down where it is cooler, so don't plan to put his kennel run on your lawn and expect it to stay a lawn.

The best bottom for the run is deep, clean sand. Some people mistakenly put down a concrete surface. This accumulates worm eggs in the concrete pores, wears the pup's hair off where his bones come closest to the surface, and gets too hot for comfort in the summer.

Gravel or cinders are even worse; they are almost impossible to keep clean. Grass also makes a poor kennel run because it soon wears out from the pup's trampling and is a frequent source of parasite contamination. The stools may not show up in the grass so you can remove them. The bare ground is much easier to keep clean.

INTRODUCING THE NEW PUPPY TO YOUR HOME

Will it harm the puppy to take him from his mother and litter mates, shut him in a dark box, and let him find himself in an entirely new environment on being taken from the box sometime afterward? Is it better to carry a puppy in one's lap in an automobile, where the pup can see what's going on and has human companionship? We can't say which is better because we don't know. Carry him home the way you prefer, because, on the basis of what we do know, it probably makes little difference. Puppies shipped by express when they are in individual crates for several days seem no worse for the experience. Puppies handled by total strangers of whom they may be at first afraid are not harmed either. When you are having a puppy sent to you, be sure to ask the shipper to use as light a crate as possible, because it is counted in figuring the weight of the pup, and the express rate is twice the cost of ordinary expressage. An orange crate with a light, solid bottom will hold most puppies.

Pet carriers made of lightweight material can be bought in any pet store. They are useful for taking puppies on the train or bus. You can find them made of aluminum, transparent plastic, heavy cardboard, and other materials suited to your pocketbook.

How old should the puppy be when he is parted from his mother? The older—preferably not less than seven weeks— the better, so far as ease of rearing goes, but most people want cute young pups, certainly not yet in the gangly adolescent stage.

Experienced people know that it pays to get the older puppy. They usually care little for cuteness. What they do realize is that the older the pup is, the fewer puppy diseases they must put up with and the easier it is to tell what he will look like when full grown.

But if you buy an older puppy, watch it carefully for signs of shyness. If the breeder has not handled it enough so that it has lost all fear of human beings it may not grow up to be as good a companion as one that has been handled a great deal from earliest puppyhood on.

THE PUPPY'S REACTION TO HIS NEW ENVIRONMENT

When you take him away from the environment to which he has become accustomed, away from his litter mates, from a small kennel, you are subjecting the puppy to a tremendous upheaval. Dogs and puppies are adaptable, and he will adapt quickly, but try to make the change as agreeable to him as possible and the least upsetting.

Don't try to make him into, or treat him like, a baby—not if you want to have as much fun as possible with your dog. Handle him as a dog right from the beginning. We see many women clients bring their puppies to our hospital swaddled in delicate fluffy woolen baby blankets and some even hold pups on their backs as if they were babies. Such treatment displays ignorance. If we figure the dog's life is one seventh that of a human being, the eight-week-old pup is equivalent to a fourteen-month-old infant. Surely no one rolls a baby of that age on its back, wraps it in blankets, and carries it about in such a manner. Then, too, the puppy is different from the human infant in that he wears his blanket. He's all dressed and can stand a good deal of cold.

Put the puppy in his pen and let him start to learn to get along in his own company. Of course he'll be lonesome. He may cry. Let him. If you hurry to him and pick him up when he cries, you are training him to cry, because he quickly learns that crying brings what he wants, and each lesson trains him to yell, perhaps more lustily. If you rush to feed him every time he cries, you are likewise training him to cry. Let him cry it out. He won't rupture himself.

Our hearts go out to the poor little lonesome mite in the kitchen or outdoors in his pen. We hear him whine and know he is crying for his mother just as a little lost pup might do if he strayed too far from home. But we also know that like all the other millions of dogs which were once puppies, he has to go through a similar ordeal. So don't sneak to the kitchen in your pajamas and begin some bad training by taking the pup back to bed with you.

Naturally you can do things to help him over his first loneliness. At night a loud-ticking alarm clock put near his bed can sometimes substitute for the heartbeat of the mother. A wad of towel sewed together to be about the size and shape of a puppy may help him. He won't use it as a toy, but to him it will feel like another pup, and he will cuddle up beside it and sleep.

Your new puppy needs a lot of watching at first and consideration too. It takes many days before all the members of the family become aware of his presence. Grandma must learn to know where the puppy is before she starts to rock in her chair. Many a delicate foot has been crushed by being rocked on.

Children, used to opening doors too fast, may bump the puppy, which may be on the other side. And everyone must watch for him when they go though swinging doors. I have known of puppies being killed when heavy doors struck them, fracturing their skulls. Swinging doors are special enemies of little puppies.

HOW TO HANDLE A PUPPY

Did you ever watch a mother dog pick up a puppy? She often takes his head in her mouth and carries him in that manner. It doesn't hurt the puppy at all. I make this statement because so many people handle a puppy, which is new to them, in the most grotesque way when trying to pick him up. When the puppy is lying down they will tenderly push the fingers and palms of both hands under him, a sort of gently shoveling him up. The puppy starts to wriggle and either falls off the hands or rolls against the body of the owner. All this is simply an imitation of a mother picking up a week-old baby.

How should you pick him up? Any firm way that is convenient, even by the tail. It won't hurt if you take hold close enough to the body. Or take a handful of head and lift him that way. He enjoys it. What he likes least is being hauled up by the loose skin on the back of the neck or by your hands under his shoulders. Of course he probably won't object while he is young, and lots of dog owners love to pick their pups up that way and sit holding them as if they were babies being coddled on the knee. There are nerve plexuses under the shoulders, and many larger puppies evince pain when the forelegs are stretched away from the body or when pressure is applied to the sensitive areas.

When you get the knack of handling a pup, picking him up becomes second nature. I'd say that the following is the best and easiest way: When he is facing the same way you are, place your right hand under the place where his breastbone ends, then lift him. He'll balance. Use your left hand to steady him if necessary.

One of the most important qualities you want to encourage in a pup is independence, and this can be done by correct handling. If you keep the pup everlastingly close to you, in your lap or with your arms around it, the puppy will usually turn out badly.

Watch the man who knows dogs. He puts the pup on a table and holds him at arm's length. He makes him stand like a dog at a dog show. When the pup squats, he raises him with a finger or two under his crotch and, with the other hand, holds its head up by upward pressure under the chin or throat. In that position he combs or brushes it, and the pup learns quickly to stand on its own four legs.

When a "hugger" takes a puppy to a veterinarian, she or he often bends over and hugs the pup on the examining table. I have had to almost pry puppies away from some owners who all but smother their pets with the false notion that the puppies like it. Puppies handled in such a manner are much more liable to have nasty dispositions than the pups who are early made to be independent, but yet have no fear of human beings.

CHILDREN AND PUPPIES

Everyone asks whether the children should be permitted to handle the new pup. Of course they should. The puppy will be all confused, but the handling won't do him any harm. Only the very young child will treat the puppy like an inanimate toy, will step on it, drop it, or hide it. Any child old enough to play with dolls can safely play with a puppy. As the puppy grows older even the smallest child can play with him, because the puppy will teach the child just how far he can go. One of my small grandsons started to carry the pet beagle puppy by one ear. It was comical to see what the puppy put up with at first, but after a few weeks the baby was showing the puppy every respect. His little plaything had asserted herself, as was her right. Soon he was carrying her around the middle; not balanced, to be sure—sometimes the front end hung lowest, sometimes the back end. A puppy lets the child know by squirming or nipping. And it is excellent education for both.

TOYS FOR THE PUPPY

Every pet shop or department store has a counter full of playthings for puppies and older dogs. Toy fire hydrants, rubber balls, rubber toy rabbits or dogs, toys with bells in them, and even rubber ones that crackle when he chews on them. These may all amuse the owner but they do not fool the dog. Practically all of these gadgets are based on the assumption that puppy owners regard puppies as babies. Mrs. Whitney, in all seriousness, tells me that women like to "play dolls" with puppies; it gives them a chance to feel motherly—something a man cannot understand. If she is correct, and she usually is, my idea of the perfect toy for a puppy is all wrong. But I am thinking of the puppy's fun, not the owner's. I am sure no finer toy for a puppy was ever devised than a big knucklebone. He will play with it by the hour, chew on it and tumble it around. However, *never* give him a bone where he can roll it in old feces, as in a dog run or on ground which may harbor worm eggs. The bone will pick up the eggs, and the puppy, in chewing or lapping at the bone, will thus become infested.

Chapter Five

FEEDING YOUR PUPPY

If your puppy is newly weaned, then he has had only his mother's milk during his first three or four weeks. This is approximately like light cream. It contains somewhere between 9 percent and 13 percent butterfat. Bottled cow's milk has only 4 percent, Holstein milk only 3 percent. On this diet, the puppy grew rapidly and plumply. At a month of age his owner probably started to feed him solid foods. Whether he did or not, the puppy's mother gave her puppies the solid food they needed. If not, then she was a most unnatural bitch. She fed her puppies in this manner: She ate her meal, waited until it was partially digested, and then regurgitated it for her offspring to eat. This is an important process that is almost always overlooked by puppy owners.

I said the new pup was newly weaned? At six or eight weeks of age, let us say, he is in a transition period. You should therefore make his food match his natural food as nearly as possible. Do not feed him unsupplemented baby food, any more than you would think of feeding a baby on puppy food. Too many puppy owners try to simulate human infant requirements. They feed them cereal foods, limewater, no fat, glucose (dextrose), and other baby foods. Indeed, judging from the elaborate feeding lists given to puppy buyers by

kennel owners, one can see they are almost copied from books
on pediatrics. About the only ingredients omitted are bananas
and mashed fruit. I've even seen orange juice, tomatoes, and
mashed carrots included in them. The thousands of cans of
baby food annually bought for puppies are a huge item—good
for puppies, to be sure, but all too expensive and unnecessary.
Let's consider sensible methods only.

THE UNWEANED PUPPY

If you've bought a puppy that has already been weaned,
then the information in the next few paragraphs will be of no
use to you. However, thousands of people annually come into
possession of unweaned pups, and since you might be one,
these paragraphs may help you.

Pan feeding

Teaching a puppy to eat or drink from a pan is more than an
academic problem. If you start right, you'll find it easy; but if
you start wrong, you will need several more days to get your
pup "on his own" at the food dish.

Three-week-old or even sixteen-day-old puppies can be
taught to lap fairly quickly. The best way to accustom them to
pan feeding is as follows: Smear some butter or cream on the
bottom of a shallow saucer and let the pup lap it off. Next place
a thin layer of warm milk in the bottom of the saucer. In drinking this, he learns to use his tongue to lap with, but he won't
be able to "dunk" his nose and become frightened. Increase
the depth of the milk with each feeding.

The way *not* to start is to fill a dish or pan with milk and
stick the puppy's nose into it. He'll surely sniff some milk up
his nose, become frightened, struggle, and thereafter be re-
pulsed by the pan. Of course you can hold his head so that he

can't jerk it downward, or with your hand around his head you can stretch his neck so that his chin makes contact with the milk's surface, thus keeping his nose out. But this method is not nearly as satisfactory and takes considerable time.

You will soon want to add bland solid food to the milk. Most of these foods tend to settle, and the puppy drinks the fluid from the top, lapping up the heavier, thicker materials last. Because the puppy will always consume the liquids before reaching the solid food, you should teach milk drinking before you offer solid food.

First solid foods

As I have said, the first solid food that a puppy eats in a natural state is game which the mother hunts, eats, partially digests, and then regurgitates. This usually adds to the puppy's diet the ingredients in which milk is low or altogether deficient, such as iron. This predigested mixture consists mostly of solid food and gives the puppies' little stomachs a greater variety to digest than the milk solids which they have had up to this time.

There are now several puppy foods available on the market any one of which may be fed with the knowledge that it is complete and will produce sound growth when fed exclusively with only water added. If you cannot find one, then buy one of the coarser foods for mature dogs, crumble it with a rolling pin, add some fat and milk, and your puppy will grow and thrive.

Among the many items, in addition to milk, on which puppies can be successfully raised for the second month are the baby foods, provided supplements are added. These include Pablum, Ceravin, canned liver, meat soups, and table scraps of the more refined sort. Big bones with some meat left, on which the puppy can gnaw, a little mashed potatoes, bread, toast, macaroni and cheese, breakfast foods, leftover meat tidbits cut reasonably small, and so forth—even a four-week-old puppy can digest these things, but milk had better be the main item of food.

Cooked eggs (but never raw eggs) are a worthwhile food for small puppies when good protein is desired. Raw or cooked liver in reasonable amounts is especially useful, and canned dog foods of the better kinds serve to add valuable nourishment. They may be fed as they come from the can or melted and made into soup.

FEEDING FOR GROWTH

Once a puppy is weaned, the food you give him makes a great difference in his development. You can cause him to grow lean and lanky or you can make him pudgy. At this time you will do well to set his eating habits for life. Not that you can't change them later, but it certainly is easier to get him used to a simple, wholesome, and complete diet from the very beginning.

I cannot overemphasize the fact that there are *systems* of dog feeding and that you should choose one of them and stick to it. If you do, you can expect much better results than if you shift from one to another. The matter of cost figures here too. Some of these systems are as follows:

1. Dry dog food and fat.
2. Canned dog food, pudding type.
3. Semi-moist food.
4. Kibbled food with supplements.
5. Table scraps.
6. Mixed; that is, any of the above with table scraps.

Dry dog food and fat

The most economical, and if the right food is chosen, the best method of puppy feeding is to buy a good dry meal-type food, mix one part edible fat to each four parts of food, add water, and feed. The dry meal costs from eight cents to fifteen cents per pound, retail, and furnishes fifteen hundred digestible calories per pound. Edible fat, such as beef fat, lard, Crisco, chicken fat, fish fat, or margarine, can be used and need cost nothing if you have enough left over from cooking. Or you can get fat trimmings from your butcher's fat barrel for five cents to eight cents per pound and add that to the meal. The fat gives you thirty-eight hundred calories per pound. There is no more economical ingredient to be found, but a puppy can digest only about 20 percent to 25 percent of fat in his diet after he is past the early mother's-milk stage. In other words, feeding fat saves money—an important consideration if you have a pup of a large breed to feed.

Canned dog food, pudding type

This is the regular canned dog food. Most of them are good, wholesome foods, but many puppies do not grow on them very well because their owners have a mistaken idea of the proper amount to feed. They are called pudding foods by the makers because they are poured as semi-liquids into the cans, but they contain so much gelatin, chondrin, and/or vegetable starches that when they cool they set into a solid mass. Observe the guarantee on each can and you will find that most of them contain from 70 percent to 75 percent moisture. This refined word for water simply means that only 25 percent to 30 percent of the content is food. In each can you get from four hundred and thirty to five hundred calories, depending on the brand. A six-month-old collie puppy requiring forty-five hundred calories a day would need ten cans daily for proper growth. In eating ten cans he would consume seven and one half pints of water, much more than he would normally drink when fed on other systems. In addition, a gallon of water to void every day would make for more difficult housebreaking.

Semi-moist food

Several companies have marketed foods which contain about 25 percent moisture usually in the form of cubes (and are packed in cellophane envelopes). They are not inexpensive. We do not know what long-term effects they may have because the preservative used in them is ordinary cane sugar of which there is about 35 percent.

For years dog owners have been warned not to feed their dogs sweets. And parents have been warned that sweets cause tooth decay in children which may or may not be true. It will be interesting to discover whether the long-continued use of the semi-moist sweet foods produce poor teeth in dogs. Ordinarily dogs do not have tooth cavities. A few rare instances have been reported. Will the sweet foods have any influence and dogs have cavities in the future? We do not know. Certainly all dogs enjoy eating the semi-moists.

Kibbled dog food with supplements

Kibbled dog foods are made from dog biscuits which have been crushed to various degrees of fineness. To my knowledge, few on the market are complete foods, and few manufacturers claim that they are. Dog biscuits are a form of unleavened bread with meat and bones in them. Some contain milk. The baking process destroys some vitamins. Dog biscuits should be looked upon as calorie suppliers—bulk—and the essential proteins and vitamins must be added. Hence meat, milk, vitamin supplements, and vegetables are usually added.

As a maintenance diet after the puppy is grown, some dog biscuits will suffice. In puppies they are useful for providing something to chew on and keeping the teeth free from tartar as the pup grows.

Kibbled biscuits are too coarse for the stomachs of very young puppies and should be well soaked before feeding. This method of feeding is an expensive one, needlessly troublesome, and not as good as the dry dog food with fat added.

Table scraps

Small-type puppies can be fed table scraps to advantage. These can include bread, potatoes, macaroni—almost all human foods, provided the starches have been cooked and mashed. Dogs gulp their food, so for years it was thought they couldn't digest starches because lumps of potato were found in their stools. Now we know that dogs can digest starches and other carbohydrates as well as we can. If you feed table scraps, be careful to see that the pup gets plenty of meat, milk, and cheese.

The table-scrap system for large dogs is one of the most expensive. It is not a matter of leftovers, as most people mistakenly think. The housewife orders more human food just as if there were another member of the family. The refrigerator no longer has tasty leftovers to put in casseroles or soup for the family. Food for human beings is costly as compared to dog foods. Remember that a growing puppy weighing forty pounds needs as much food a day as a 190-pound man.

The mixed diet

This usually consists of table scraps, dog biscuits, and canned dog food. It can be complete and usually is. Puppies grow well on it, but generally are spoiled. The rascals decide what they like best and refuse other foods perhaps better for them. If you feed this way, mix the ingredients thoroughly in every meal.

As I said previously, get a system and stick to it. While a puppy is growing and hungry enough to eat almost anything, you can shape his lifelong eating habits. You don't have to worry about what he will eat and what he won't. Keep him on the hungry side. Refuse to be his slave; keep him yours, and he'll love you better for it.

Don't worry about variety. The puppy doesn't need it or crave it so long as he has a complete diet. He can smell each of the ingredients of which his food is composed—a feat impossible for us. He gets variety in each meal.

IS HE GROWING FAST ENOUGH?

Everyone raising a puppy asks this at one time or another. In order to help you answer this question, a table has been

SATISFACTORY WEEKLY WEIGHT GAINS FROM SIX WEEKS OF AGE TO FULL GROWN

BREED WEIGHT GROUP POUNDS	WEEKLY GAIN POUNDS	OUNCES
5 to 10		6
15 to 20		12
25 to 30	1	2
35 to 40	1	10
45 to 50	2	0
55 to 60	2	5
65 to 70	2	1
75 to 80	3	0
85 to 90	3	4
95 to 100	3	8
105 to 110	3	12
115 to 120	4	0
125 to 130	4	4
135 to 140	4	8
145 to 150	4	12
155 to 160	5	0
165 to 170	5	4

included showing what I consider excellent weekly growth in puppies.

The gains are average because they represent not the growth of one dog in a breed, but in some cases, of as many as twenty litters. I have omitted the weights of weak and backward puppies because I wanted these gains to be a standard by which you can compare the growth of your puppy. You may find that yours has done as well as or much better than many of mine. I have tried to make the gains represent an average, so that, if your puppies grow as fast, you may be sure they are prospering.

HOW OFTEN TO FEED

After weaning (approximately seven weeks), a puppy can do very well on three meals a day. It is important to get him accustomed to a diet regime during his growing period, when he is always hungry.

After he reaches six months of age his stomach will have enlarged, and he will grow satisfactorily on two meals a day. When a puppy has consumed enough food he shows it by his bulging belly. This bulge does not mean he will have a sagging belly after he is grown; it will shrink as his appetite diminishes with the cessation of growth.

By the eighth month one meal a day is enough for any dog, although you may split the one meal up into two feedings if you wish. Remember that a healthy mature dog will eat 25 percent to 50 percent more than he needs; don't yield to the temptation to overfeed. Always keep your dog somewhat hungry, and don't feed him unless he is hungry. A good rule is not to feed him at all unless he is hungry enough to greedily eat a piece of dry bread.

AGE OF FULL GROWTH BY BREEDS

There is still a great difference of opinion on the question of what constitutes full growth. For example, if you ask the breeders of Great Danes when these dogs become full grown, some will tell you at ten months, and others will say at three years.

Growth does not just mean gaining weight. Lots of puppies stop growing and then become heavier by simply filling out their frames with fat or larger muscles. The kind of growth that we are considering here is the general skeletal growth, regardless of the amount of fat the puppy accumulates.

There are characteristic breed and strain traits that cause some puppies to grow differently from others, just as one type of child grows differently from another. We all know people who never were fat and who never will be fat, and we know others who grew up as fat, pudgy children and who, at adolescence, became slim and lost all the childhood pudginess. In the same way, there are English setters that grow up into slim puppies and fail to become heavy with fat at any time during their growing period, while some chow dogs are plump, under their woolly coats, all during their growth on the same diet.

When I talk about the attainment of full growth, I mean that the *skeleton* has practically finished its growth. This attainment is coincident with a great diminution of the appetite. Your puppy, which perhaps has been eating three pounds of a mixture of food a day, will suddenly eat only one pound and three ounces. In fact, this cessation is often so abrupt that you may think your dog is sick. At this point, too, you may find an actual drop in the weight curve, but the curve comes back to normal quickly and may even creep up because of fat accretion.

Very few bitches will come in heat before they are full

grown, so the age at sexual maturity is sometimes used as a gauge of growth completion. Questionnaires returned from a large number of breeders show their estimate of the age of first heat. Being full grown does not cause a bitch to come in heat; the point is that bitches come in heat at the following ages (see table), and therefore growth was probably complete before that time.

There may be a slight growth beyond this point in some dogs. Representatives of the very large breeds show it more than the smaller type of dog. I know of two Great Danes that actually grew in height until they were twenty-seven months old. This growth was skeletal growth by actual measurement.

There are two characteristics of rapid growth that cause special concern to owners of large-breed puppies. I refer to the development of heavy bones, especially the knob that appears at the wrist joint; owners are sure this is a sign of rickets. It is only a sign of excellent development. The other oddity is the tendency of large puppies, if not all puppies, to grow taller behind than in front. At seven months of age, the front legs seem much too short, and the puppy appears improperly developed. Many measurements of growing pups convince me that this is the normal expectation and that late in the growth period the front leg growth catches up so the puppy appears in perfect balance. I have seen Great Danes two inches too short in front at the tenth month, and by the twelfth month they have grown the two inches.

Do we gain anything by forcing our dogs to make very rapid growth? We avoid criticism, possibly, because a great many people think that if a dog isn't growing at breakneck speed he's slowly dying. Actually, much research on other species and a little done on dogs shows that slow growth probably tends to make the animal live longer and be somewhat more resistant to certain diseases, generally tougher than the animal

BREEDS	AGE AT FIRST HEAT MONTHS
Sight hounds (all breeds)	11
Greyhounds	
Salukis	
Afghans	
Giants	
Great Danes	10
Mastiffs	10
Newfoundlands	11
Irish wolfhounds	15
Russian wolfhounds	12
Scottish deerhounds	15
Saint Bernards	16
Shepherds (all breeds)	10
Bulldogs (all breeds)	10
Terriers	
All small breeds	8
Airedale	9
Bird Dogs (all breeds)	10
Setters	
Pointers	
Retrievers	
Springer spaniels	
Cocker spaniels	
Others	
Toys	7–8
Pekingese	
Pomeranians	
Miniature poodles	
Others	
Miscellaneous	
Chow	7
Doberman	10
Boxer	10
Samoyed	8
Eskimo	11
Dalmatian	9
Elkhound	9

that is grown at breakneck speed. However, not all of the evidence is in on this question, by any means.

If students of nutrition were certain that slow growth was more desirable than rapid growth, they might be alarmed by the fact that our boys and girls grow much faster now than they did a generation ago. Among the dogs whose growth I forced faster than any I have ever known before or since, there are a great many still alive that are healthy, and some of them have lived to over twelve. It is my general impression from limited experimentation that they have lived as long as the slower-growing ones.

There is a great difference of opinion as to whether pushing a dog to grow rapidly will make him a larger dog than his litter mates which are grown more slowly. Some years ago I felt definitely that it made no difference whatever. Since then I have had an opportunity to make a careful study, using two consecutive litters of bloodhounds from the same parents. One litter was pushed as rapidly as possible and was full grown in seven and a half months. Puppies in the other litter, fed only one meal a day, took eighteen months to reach full growth. Comparison between them was quite startling. The first litter weighed from ninety to one hundred and nine pounds each; the second ranged from seventy-two to eighty-five pounds each. Curiously enough, the larger ones also seemed to have better bloodhound characteristics.

Breeders of Newfoundlands, Saint Bernards, Great Danes, and other large breeds tell me they think rapid growth is conducive to greater size. But on this question, also, not all the evidence is in. We need many carefully controlled studies on this subject.

RETARDED GROWTH

Suppose now that your puppy, which has been growing well, loses his appetite, or eats and yet does not grow. What can be the cause? It might be one of many:

1. Disease.
2. Intestinal parasites.

3. Lice.

4. Teething. If you keep weight records of your puppy's growth, do not worry when, at about fifteen weeks of age, he suddenly loses weight or fails to grow. Almost every puppy has a setback at teething time. Look in his mouth and probably you will find several loose teeth. Eating is painful during teething. This is an explosive phenomenon compared with the slow teething of children. It will be over in six weeks, and it will take the puppy a week or so to get used to sore gums; then he will be his young self again.

5. Changes of diet, which we have already discussed.

6. Poison. Puppies love to lap or chew things, and sometimes they swallow or burn their mouths with substances like paint, spray materials, rat poison, "ant buttons," "mouse seed," roach poison, warfarin. In that case appetite fails, weight diminishes, and the puppy may die, or he may linger on in a pathetic state for weeks. Sometimes the kidneys and liver are damaged. Burns, inside or out, heal slowly. Don't expect a rapid recovery when a pup has been poisoned.

7. Foreign bodies in the stomach or intestines. I have picked up many puppies and heard stones rattling together in their stomachs. Most people who have raised a considerable number of puppies can relate experiences of losing pups because of stones or other foreign bodies lodged in their intestines. I have operated and removed dozens and have lost a few fine puppies of my own.

8. Intussusceptions. It is quite common to find a long area of telescoped intestine in well-cared-for pups. I have known clients' puppies to live for three weeks, entirely unable to digest food, in some pain, and, of course, losing weight. Surgery saved them.

If your pup fails to gain, appears in pain, out of sorts, and does not become hungry in a few days, consult your veterinarian. And of course, if he is poisoned, rush him to the veterinarian after giving first aid at home (Chapter Six).

DEBUNKING NOTIONS

In this day of scientific liberation from foolish superstitions, it is strange how many of the old foolish notions still persist and that puppies are still suffering from them. Here are a few to forget:

Milk makes worms. If this were so, why feed it to one's children? Worms come from eggs, and milk has no worm eggs.

Sweets make worms. No. Sweets spoil the appetite for more wholesome food, that's all.

A dog must have fresh, lean meat. Three errors are here. He can live well with no meat at all, fat meat is good for him but not necessary; the meat can be frozen, dried, cooked, and doesn't need to be fresh.

Bones are necessary for sound teeth. Not bones, but what bones contain, are necessary. And all good prepared foods contain plenty of ground bone.

Garlic in food kills worms. It doesn't, so don't waste time and money on it.

Dogs can't digest potatoes. If potatoes are in lumps, dogs, who generally gulp their food, will swallow the lumps whole, but if you mash the cooked potatoes, puppies can digest them as well as we do.

Fats are indigestible by dogs. No diet with less than 15 percent fat can be considered balanced. Hard-working dogs can digest up to 70 percent of fat in their diets. Sedentary puppies handle 20 percent very well.

Meat makes dogs vicious. Absurd!

Cooked meat is better than raw. Nutritionally, no, but in the case of pork, cooking kills the parasites it may contain.

Chapter Six

YOUR PUPPY'S HEALTH

Cleaning, grooming, immunization, and sanitation against diseases are all matters of health. You will probably want to leave many health matters to your veterinarian, but you will have no desire to make unnecessary calls. This chapter will help you to know when to go see your dog's doctor and what facts to ascertain before you see him.

PART ONE

"DISTEMPER"

A generation ago any disease which produced symptoms of sniffling and loss of appetite was called distemper. Veterinary scientists have unraveled this distemper complex, as it is now called and found that it consists of many diseases. Some veterinarians refer to one of these diseases—namely, Carré's disease —as distemper.

IMMUNIZATION

It is most important that you find out, if you can, what sort of "shots" have been given your puppy before you owned him.

That word "shots" might mean anything, so if you hear from the seller that the pup had his "puppy shots," don't be content with that, because your veterinarian will ask you, "Did he have serum or vaccine, live or dead? Was he protected against distemper or Carré's disease, hardpad disease, infectious hepatitis?" Be prepared to tell him. Perhaps the puppy had dual serum—that is, serum which temporarily protects against Carré's disease and hepatitis. Insist that the seller be specific.

These are the diseases against which your puppy can and, in my opinion, should be vaccinated: Carré's disease, hardpad disease, infectious canine hepatitis. Following are their symptoms, which are given for several purposes: first, to help you to recognize the disease; secondly, to alert you so you will have your puppy protected. It is better to be so much alarmed at the possibilities that you will be moved into action to prevent your puppy from ever having one of these killing or maiming diseases than to simply drift and wait until he gets one and then try to cure him. And it is far less expensive, too, to say nothing of saving hours of care and heartache.

Carré's disease

This disease that some still call "distemper" has undoubtedly killed millions of dogs in the past, but its incidence is greatly reduced now.

Symptoms. The incubation period is five days. Temperature rises to about 103.5 degrees in puppies. The first noticeable symptoms are shunning of light (photophobia), a pain in the eyes from light, and vomiting. The next day, the sixth, the pup appears normal. On the seventh day the eyes and nose start to discharge, the bowels loosen. He coughs with a dry hacking cough. Day by day the nasal and optic discharge become thicker and more abundant. The eyes crust over, the nose runs ropes of nasty mucus. The bowel evacuation is thinner, dark, and sometimes bloody, with a horrible odor which is so pervasive that a whole room will be filled with it. When this disease was prevalent years ago, one could almost tell by the smell that the pup had the disease.

In addition, the appetite disappears, the pup loses weight rapidly and becomes dehydrated, as you can tell from the way his skin stands in a fold when you lift it up. Sometimes the eyes turn blue from the pus; often the eyeball seems etched away.

Some older dogs recover from Carré's disease. Most puppies die, although pups of some breeds are more resistant. Many die of brain inflammation after they seem almost well.

Pneumonia is a usual accompaniment, but this can be cured by antibiotics.

Once a puppy contracts this disease, there is usually little hope of curing him. Therefore you must protect him just as all of us were protected against smallpox.

Prevention. There are a dozen ways of immunizing against Carré's disease. Your veterinarian may prefer a different one than that which I will recommend. He may even want to give a series of temporary doses of serum and later a series of doses of vaccine.

After having immunized more than seven thousand puppies and dogs within twenty-four months at the Whitney Veterinary Clinic and noted the wonderful immunity the following method has given, this is our standard procedure for dog breeders who own litters. At the age of four to eight weeks puppies of small breeds are given half a dose of Lederle's Cabvac vaccine, puppies of large breeds a full dose. When these puppies reach five months of age we give all of them another dose of the full amount. We have never seen a break.

Of course most of the puppies brought to us for vaccination are weaned—eight to ten weeks old or older. We tell our clients to keep the pups segregated from all other dogs until they are ten weeks old, and then we give them a full dose, which our experience shows apparently immunizes them solidly. There is no need for a series of "shots"—just one, which costs less and is effective not only against Carré's disease, but against hardpad disease, which we shall consider next.

"Puppy Shots." This meaningless term has become a by-word among puppy owners. Usually these owners have no idea what it means. More often than not, a series of injections of serum has been given by a veterinarian, and the serum afforded temporary protection. Each immunizing dose lasts about eleven days, according to Laidlaw and Dunkin, who invented the serum. But the doses are generally given three weeks apart. If permanent immunity is to be given, a considerable time must elapse after the last dose of serum or there may be enough protection in the body to neutralize the vaccine. During this crucial time your puppy is not protected.

So one wonders why puppies are not given permanent or, at worst, semi-permanent immunity while they are little and at a great saving.

Hardpad disease

During each of the years 1952 and 1953 we at the Whitney Veterinary Clinic saw over a thousand puppies die from hard-pad disease, and certainly not over two dozen came down with Carré's disease during both years. In your section these proportions may be reversed. Had these puppies been properly immunized, we would have seen no disease.

Symptoms. Hardpad disease has a longer incubation period than Carré's disease, shows no pronounced symptoms, but produces some mucus in the eyes and very little from the nose.

The appetite is sporadic, and there is a slight cough. The stools may be a little loose, but in general are almost normal.

The distinguishing characteristic of this disease is the hardening and thickening of the pads of the feet. Sometimes the pads will be rounded, but more often flat. They may grow so hard they become like bone; you can hear a dog walking on concrete or tile walks. It sounds as though he had marbles instead of rubbery toes.

The temperature hovers around 103.5 degrees. The disease lasts about three weeks after noticeable symptoms are seen. One day the owner will notice that the pads are starting to crack or soften around the edges. At just about this time the pup has his first convulsion, or twitch, or some other manifestation of encephalitis; the virus has invaded the brain.

Dogs that recover usually are left with twitches.

Prevention. Only one method of immunization against hardpad disease has as yet been successful—namely, the avianized virus made by the Lederle Laboratories. The older method of vaccine dosage, while it protected against Carré's disease, did not protect against hardpad; whereas the former, which is more efficient and requires only one injection, is also less expensive.

Infectious canine hepatitis

This is another disease which used to pass as distemper, but it is as much unlike Carré's disease as human hepatitis is unlike smallpox. Research shows that it is a different disease from the human hepatitis, not transmissible from one species to another.

Canine hepatitis frightens puppy owners because it is most severe in its effects upon puppies. An infected pup may appear well one day and be dead the next. Grown dogs very seldom die of it. However, any dogs that survive may have impaired vision and may be sterile. When dogs survive you may observe one or both of the eyes turning bluish white. This is because the virus damages the outside layers. Hepatitis virus may permanently destroy some of the delicate retina in the back of the eye. The white color of the transparent front of the eye usually clears in a week.

Symptoms. As already stated, the ravages of hepatitis are often disastrous. Pups that live two days often recover, but have a protracted illness of varying severity. Older puppies that live one day after the first symptoms seldom die. The temperature averages 104–105 degrees.

Those puppies that survive the first few days may cough because their tonsils usually swell. The eyes water, and the nose runs with a clear watery substance. The stool is loose and sometimes shows blood.

Prevention. An efficient vaccine which gives long protection against hepatitis can be administered by your veterinarian. It may be given separately or at the same time as the Carré vaccination. If there is any doubt about possible exposure during the week that the puppy is building up immunity, your pup's doctor can give some duo-serum along with the other two and in that way provide temporary and permanent protection at the same time.

Leptospirosis

This is the disease that in my opinion is more dangerous than any other. I think so because it is one of the few diseases of dogs that is contagious to human beings. It may leave the victim with weakened heart and kidneys, and there is much more of it among dogs and ourselves than is commonly realized. The cause is a spiral-shaped bacterium. It is believed to be spread to dogs by urine—either dog or rat urine. The short-legged breeds seem to have it more often than the longer legged, possibly because the bacterium can enter the body via the penis and vulva. This is a good reason for keeping dogs, puppies or mature dogs away from puddles where other dogs' urine could contaminate the water.

Actually there are two forms, one much more severe than the other. The form that goes by the long name of *Leptospira icterohaemorrhagica* causes Weil's Disease in man and jaundice and hemorrhages in dogs. The milder form is called the *Canicola* and is frequently inaccurately diagnosed because the symptoms are milder.

Symptoms of Canicola Form. The temperature is elevated sometimes to 105 degrees, but more often to 103 degrees. The puppy vomits, loses appetite and weight, passes loose stools, and appears stiff in its muscular movements. One constant symptom is the congestion of the blood vessels in the whites of the eyes. In severe cases the urine may be so tinged with yellow that it is orange colored and even chocolate brown.

The icterohaemorrhagic form produces the same symptoms but in addition, jaundice is exhibited early in all the visible mucous membranes. The whites of the eyes turn yellow, the inside of the lips are orange, and finally the skin yellows. The puppy passes blood in its stools, and may vomit blood.

Prevention. Your veterinarian can vaccinate your puppy or puppies with a dual-purpose vaccine which immunizes against both forms of the disease. This can be done at the same time the puppy is given his Carré's (distemper) and hepatitis vaccines, all in one injection—a great boon to every puppy and its owner.

Treatment. Should your puppy show symptoms, your veterinarian can give heavy doses of one of the tetracycline drugs with excellent expectation of saving its life. If the heart and kidneys have been damaged, it won't show up until past middle life, which is the best possible reason for having the puppy protected early.

Rabies

While rabies can destroy puppies it is found principally in grown dogs. In states where vaccination against it is compulsory, rabies is a menace. Have your puppy vaccinated by the time he is six months old and younger if there has been a case near you. In rabies-free states there is not much sense in such vaccination. It must be repeated once a year.

DISEASES WITH NO IMMUNIZATION

There are many other puppy diseases that you can recognize, but against which, as yet, we have no means of conferring immunity. Here, in brief, are symptoms to watch for that will alert you to danger. Let's hope your puppy never shows one symptom, and is never sick a day in his life.

Pneumonia

A great many puppies, even in warm weather, develop pneumonia from a variety of causes.

Symptoms. The temperature is high—104 degrees or more. The eyes and nose usually exude mucus. The puppy may cough and wheeze. If you hold your ear to his chest, the rasping breathing is clearly audible. It is so easy to mistake pneumonia for several other diseases of the distemper complex that it is advisable to let your veterinarian handle the case should your pup become ill. Also, since the antibiotic drugs cure it so efficiently, and each is a prescription drug, a call on your veterinarian is inevitable.

Other diseases of the distemper complex

Coccidiosis, tonsillitis, and toxoplasmosis, are all diseases whose symptoms are confusing, and all cause sniffling. Your puppy could have any one. Only one, coccidiosis, is not amenable to treatment. Early treatment of any disease is more successful, so go to see your veterinarian at the first sign of sickness. He may not be able to tell in one visit what the disease is, but he may give an antibiotic and abort the sickness before its severe symptoms set in, in which case you will never be certain what disease the puppy actually had. If the disease is caused by a virus, don't expect too much help. Drugs are of no avail, and if serum is given, it is expensive, and only huge doses have any effect.

SKIN DISEASES

Besides the insects we shall consider later, puppies' skin falls victim to several kinds of disease. We shall not attempt to classify them here, but a few are eczema, moist and dry (a very inexact connotation), ringworm, dandruff, and a general catchall term of summer skin disease.

Nobody knows the exact causes of all of these diseases, but because most of them (ringworm excepted) appear in the hot, moist part of the year and tend to disappear in the cold, dry part, the probably correct assumption is that they are caused by that class of invisible microscopic organisms called fungi. At any rate, a large number of different fungi have been isolated from dogs' skin, but the same ones have been isolated from healthy skin.

Fleabites play a large role in admitting disease organisms, but how large a role no one knows. Certainly research evidence indicates that when fleas are not present on one group of dogs they will have less skin disease than another group infested with fleas, even when both groups are kept together. Depending on the kind of skin infection, we find puppies showing these symptoms—nervousness, scratching for no apparent reason, nibbling at their skin, and a peculiar pungent odor in some infections.

In *ringworm,* which is contagious to human beings and more often is given to the dog by our species than contracted from them by us, roundish bald spots appear. Itching causes the dog to scratch or nibble at the skin. The irritation and moisture may produce a scab. The final product is a smooth oval or round bare spot which eventually clears up and hairs out.

The moist variety of *eczema* may appear almost anywhere, but especially on the sides of the face, on the back, and frequently on the thighs. It is much more likely to be seen on long-haired dogs. This type seems to appear overnight as a wet nasty spot, and usually the skin is thickened from the pup's chewing or scratching.

In dry eczema the affected area is much larger, and one does not find it appearing suddenly. First indications are a general loss of hair in the infected area, which is usually along the back near the tail. One finds denuded areas also behind the hind legs and on the tail. If this infection is neglected too long, the skin on the back will thicken, and odor characteristic of the disease becomes quite pervasive.

Dandruff is simply the shedding off of the outer layer of skin. It is not a sign of disease. All dogs show some dandruff, but only in older puppies is it pronounced. In the opinion of some students the addition of fat to the diet ends excessive dandruff, but this is questionable. Thorough brushing gets it out of the coat.

Cradle cap is what some people call the little pimples which appear on the skin of young puppies. Almost any skin remedy —even lard and sulphur—dries them up and cures the skin. A severe case causes much itching and considerable redness of the skin.

Scratching for No Apparent Reason. There is never any

scratching without cause, but sometimes it is difficult to find the cause. If your puppy scratches, here is how you can generally find the trouble:

Start at the head. Look in the ears. Smell them. If necessary, clean them out with a good ear lotion which will dissolve the wax and kill the germs. Your veterinarian can supply you with one.

Look all over the body for fleas and especially for lice, which can often be detected by the white shiny nits stuck to hairs.

If you can't find a single "passenger" on the pup, start to feel. Since you can't see through the puppy's hair, feeling will usually detect small bumps or scales somewhere. It takes only one tiny pimplelike infection center to make a puppy scratch as if he itched everywhere on his body. Feel beside the tail in the folds of the skin. Feel the hind legs, where he sits and his skin comes in contact with the ground. These are the places he may be infected.

Pay no attention to where he scratches, because all he has to have is one flea nibbling at his thigh and he may be scratching at his shoulder. Where he nibbles at his skin is a better place to look, because then he is more accurate in locating the trouble.

The Relation of Food and Skin Diseases. You can practically forget food as a cause of skin diseases. Almost all of the skin diseases are external infections, so far as any reliable research indicates. Once in a great while you may find your puppy's face swollen and lumps as large as a quarter sticking up all over his body. This rare condition is probably brought about by the puppy having eaten some bacterial toxin—usually a partly spoiled egg. I have seen it come from a robin's egg, duck egg, and in many cases from hens' eggs. But this is not a skin disease.

Constant shedding is not necessarily a sign of disease. Some older puppies shed hair constantly. All of them have one good shedding season sometime during their first year. There is no way to control this condition except to regulate their hours of daylight and darkness to correspond with natural conditions. The lengthening of the day causes natural shedding, and the shortening of the day causes the new luxuriant coat to come in. You can't expect to have a non-shedding coat on your pup if he is kept inside with the same number of hours of light the year round. And that is the condition we achieve by turning on the lights when it gets dark outside. Electric lights have the same effect on the puppy as daylight. We have to put up with some shedding and use a comb to remove the surplus hair.

Mange. See Part Two of this chapter.

Treatment of Skin Diseases. In the treatment of skin diseases there have been many remedies which were effective, some more efficacious against one form than another. Your veterinarian can supply you with the best one for the specific form of skin disease that he finds your pup to have.

INTESTINAL DISORDERS

We have already seen that several diseases can be counted on to produce loose stools, but many other diseases can produce the same results. Parasites, especially coccidiosis, come first to mind, but there are many germ infections which, if caught in time, can be eradicated, and the character of the stools can be changed overnight. The layman has almost no way of determining which infections are serious and which are not. My experience shows that more often than not laymen give the wrong medicines because of incorrect diagnosis. All diarrheas, with the exception of food diarrhea, are serious; leave the diagnosis to your veterinarian.

Some diets are naturally laxative. If your puppy ate too much fat or a large bowl of skim milk or a raw egg, or food with bran, for example, you must expect his stool to be loose. A normal puppy under three months of age, depending upon the character of the diet, defecates about six to eight times a day, and because his whole rate of digestion is speeded up over that of a mature dog, his bowel movements are softer.

If your puppy needs only more constipating foods, these will usually help: boiled whole milk, cottage cheese, hard-boiled egg, meat, boiled polished rice. Sometimes the addition of a small amount of fat to the diet slows up the passage of food and firms the stools. If more than 20 percent (dry weight) of fat is fed, the stools may be gray and too soft.

Looseness of the bowel movement can be due to a variety of causes. If your puppy develops it, consider the following, and try to place the cause. If it is something simple, which you can correct, do it; if not, consult your veterinarian. Here are some of the causes:

Food. Change in diet often causes a change in the bacteria that fill the digestive tract, which in turn, causes a temporary diarrhea. Feeding laxative foods, such as bran flakes, skim milk, raw eggs of which only the yolk is digested, the white slithering through the stomach mostly undigested, fruit, et cetera, causes loose stools.

Exercise. When taken for a romp, a puppy used to small quarters almost always starts voiding loose stools within a few minutes. But then so do mature dogs.

Fright. A badly frightened puppy may pass a solid stool, followed by considerable diarrhea.

Generalized Diseases. Accompanying almost all of the general sicknesses of puppies—Carré's disease, hardpad, hepatitis, leptospirosis, and others—is looseness of the stool. It should be a signal to you to consult your veterinarian unless you know the specific cause.

Parasites. In mild infestations the stools may be normal, but in heavy infestations the stools may be even watery. This is particularly true of coccidiosis.

It is wise, therefore, to let your veterinarian study the puppy's stool at the sign of persistent diarrhea. If correcting the diet or reducing the exercise does not check it, then let the doctor see what he can do. Paregoric will stop diarrhea and make the puppy sleepy, but it will not remove the cause. The usual mixtures of kaolin, pectin, and other drugs may produce a temporary effect, but cure nothing; we call them palliatives. Your veterinarian can give you antibiotics to destroy the organisms that cause the disease. But don't expect him to cure virus diseases; they can only be prevented, not cured.

DEFICIENCY DISEASES

Rickets

True *rickets,* a disease due to a lack of calcium, phosphorus, or vitamin D, shows up as crooked bones in the forearm or by wrist joints which bend in or out.

It is just as important to realize what similar conditions are not rickets. Weak front legs are not necessarily rickety. A large development of the end of the radius (the larger bone in the forearm) at the wrist joint usually is a good indication that the pup will be a large dog. It is not a sign of rickets. A puppy kept in a wet place may develop such weak wrist joints that he seems to be on skis. He may actually walk on his wrist joints. But this is not rickets. Neither is a foot with sprawly toes that look like fingers.

A puppy which "knuckles over" does not have rickets, and

Afghan

Beagle

Basset Hound

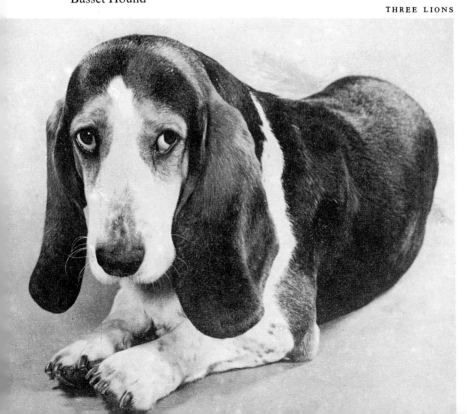

Bloodhound

AKE WINTZELL

Bedlington

WM. BROWN, COURTESY OF WM. A. ROCKEFELLER,
ROCK RIDGE KENNELS

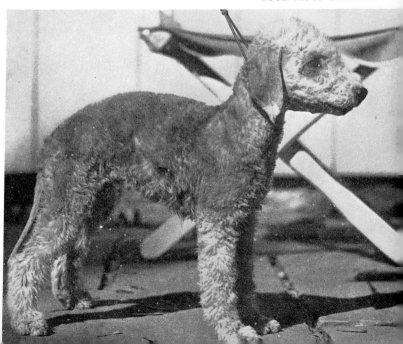

Bulldog

Boxer

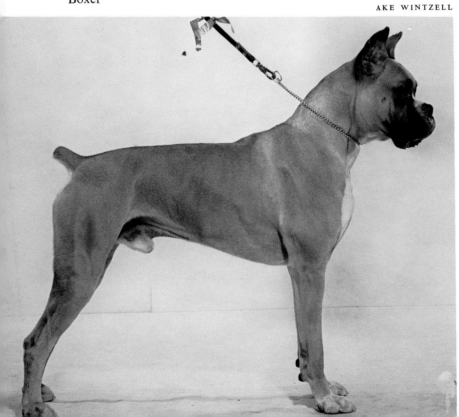

Boston Terrier

Chihuahua,
short-haired

Chihuahua, long-haired

Cocker Spaniel

Cocker Spaniel, woolly

Collie

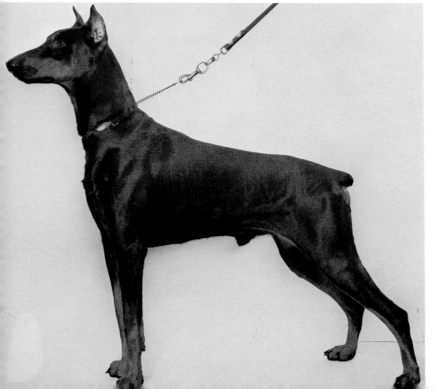

Dachshund

Dalmatians

Doberman Pinscher

English Setter

German Shepherd

COURTESY OF E. H. FAUSETTE, ROCHESTER, N.Y.

Golden Retriever

Great Dane

Greyhound

Irish Setter

Irish Wolfhound

Labrador Retriever

Pointer

Poodle, Toy

Pekingese

Redbone Coonhound

Schipperke

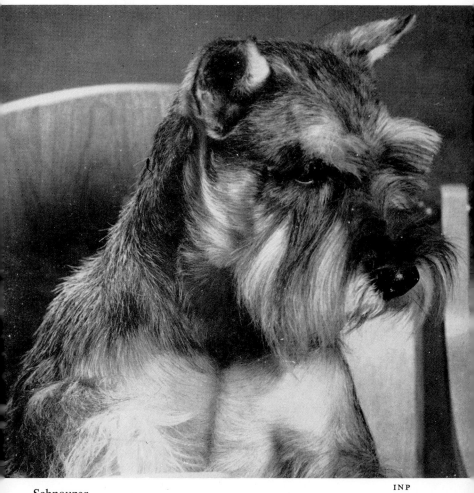

Schnauzer

Scottie

Weimaraners

Welsh Terrier

Simple Commands

Start with a hungry pup. Let him nibble at the reward you will use.

When he paws at your hand, say "shake" and then give him the reward. Repeat as often as necessary until he associates "shake" with the desired action.

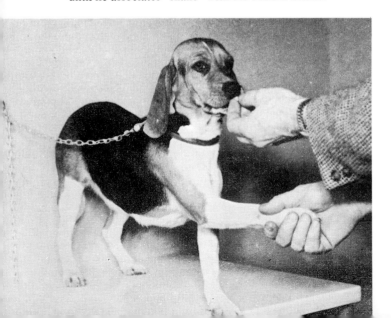

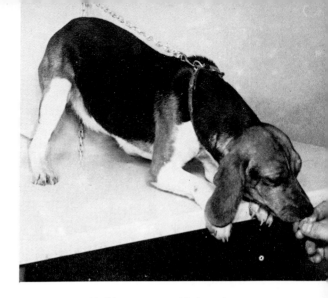

Hold your reward below the table top. He will then have to lie down to reach it. Say "lie down" and reward him. Then stand him up and repeat until he reacts to the words.

To make him stand up, hold the reward high and say "up." Use this to follow the command "lie down."

Getting Your Dog to Use the Leash

Start with a hungry dog. Apply the leash—the dog
will struggle briefly. Let him know that you have
food for him and let him nibble from your fingers.

Now coax him along so that he realizes that there
is pressure on his neck. When he associates the
reward with the neck pressure, he will shortly
forget the collar and leash and walk along with you.

Picking Up and Holding Your Puppy

Never pick your puppy up this way
(though its mother might).

The correct way to pick up a
small puppy.

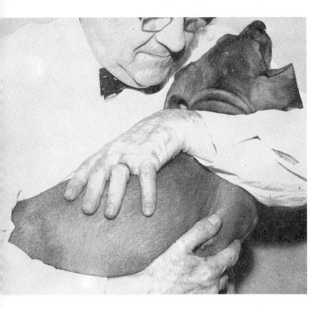

Never hold a large puppy this way—it's uncomfortable.

This ten-week-old Redbone Hound is correctly held.

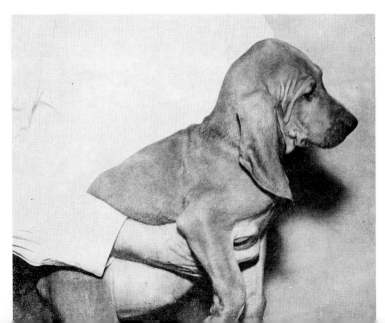

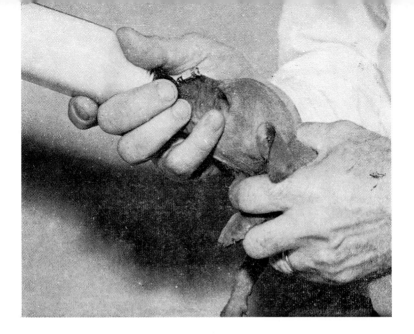

Feeding Your Puppy

Feeding the "orphan" pup.

Note the hypodermic needle in the nipple which acts as an air valve.

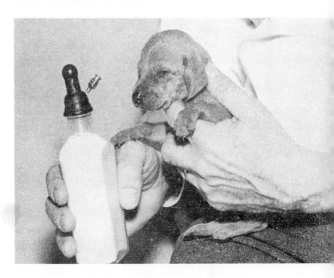

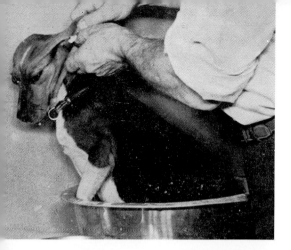

Bathing Your Dog

Fill the ear canal with a wad of cotton.

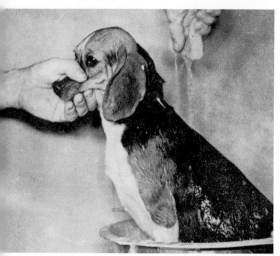

Soap and wet the coat.

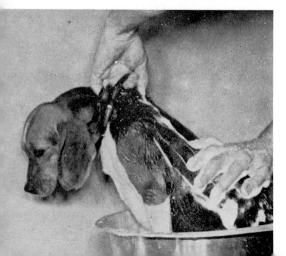

Lather well.

Rinse and squeeze the surplus soap from the coat.

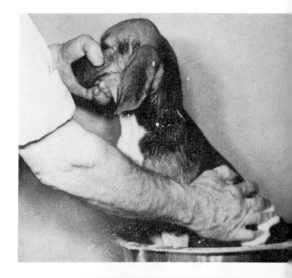

Pour on the deodorant and and insecticide rinse. Don't forget to wash the collar!

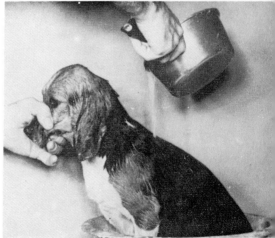

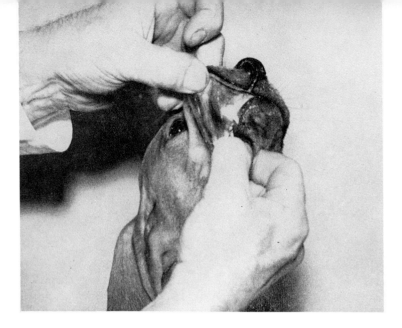

Giving Medicine

To dose a dog with a liquid—pull out the
lips to make a pocket.

Have someone slowly pour in the medicine.

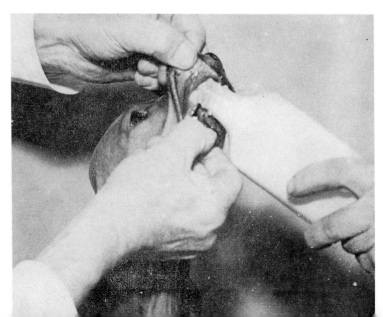

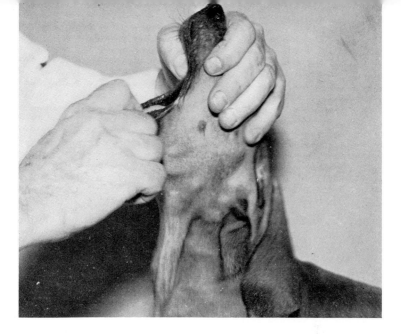

To administer a pill or capsule, hold the lips around the upper teeth, pull down the lower jaw, and drop the pill or capsule on the back of the tongue.

With index finger push the pill or capsule down to China!

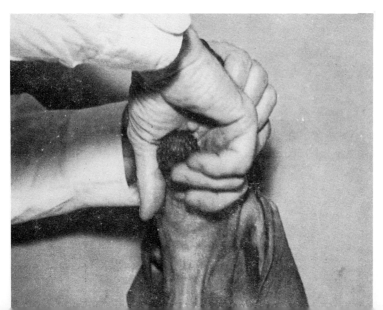

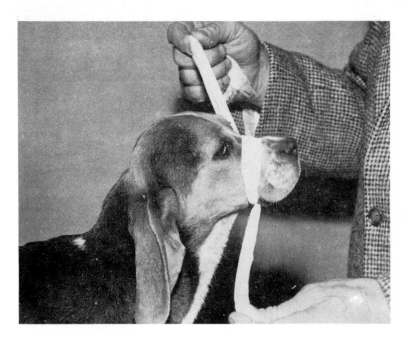

Applying a Mouth Tie

Before treating an injured dog it is necessary to apply a mouth tie. Using strips of cloth (*not* string), encircle dog's muzzle.

Then draw under and behind dog's ears and tie firmly.

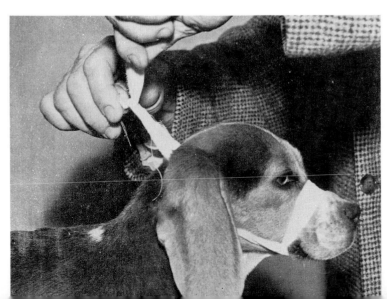

Clipping the Nails

Clipping the dog's nails with
ordinary shears.

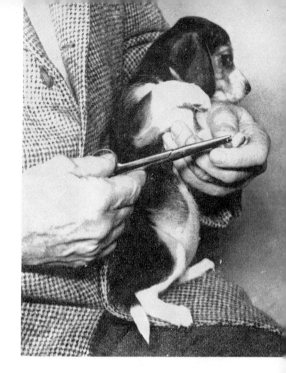

The Whelping Bed

Arrange straw in the shape
of a shallow bowl, to keep the
puppies near the mother.

Dog Runs and Wire Bottom Pens

A manufactured puppy pen with wire floor—useful for indoor puppy raising. *Courtesy of Keene Supply Co.*

Outdoor pens with wire floor and closed-in hutch at the back.

he usually outgrows the condition in a few weeks. You can tell whether your puppy has rickets by knowing what you feed him. If he eats any of the better grades of meal or biscuits, if he gets milk or ground bone in his diet, the chances are that his weak legs, if he has them, are not a sign of rickets.

A drop or two a day of percomorph oil (*oleum perco-morphum*) and some ground bone will prevent rickets and cure the defect if the bones have not become bent.

Vitamin-A deficiency

Before more careful studies were made on its total effects, it was the custom to dose puppies (and babies) with cod-liver oil. This was done to provide vitamins A and D. It is quite probable that more harm than good has been done by such dosing. The oil of cod livers is toxic; the vitamins are essential. Children are no longer fed cod-liver oil. When A and D vitamins are needed, doctors may prescribe percomorph oil, an enormously rich concentrate containing about sixty thousand units of vitamin A and eight thousand units of vitamin D in each drop. One drop a day is enough for any young puppy.

But when should your puppy be given any? Perhaps never, especially if he is fed synthetic vitamins A and D. If you feed any of the good meal-type foods, he gets all he needs of both.

If he is stunted, has sore eyes, is night-blind, deaf, has a scaly skin, or if his movements are uncoordinated, he may have vitamin-A deficiency. If he has coccidiosis, by all means see that he has several drops of percomorph oil a day. But no one can look at a sick pup and say, "He needs vitamin A." No one, that is, who doesn't know what you have fed your puppy.

Vitamin-B-complex deficiency

This rare ailment need never trouble your puppy if you give good meal-type food and milk. The symptoms of severe

B-complex deficiency are nervousness, irritability, loss of weight, staggering gait, paralysis, sore mouth. A teaspoonful of brewer's yeast given daily will prevent it completely. One of the B-complex factors, B_{12}, is especially concerned with growth. But since it is associated with animal proteins, such as meat, fish, liver, milk, whether fresh or dried, few puppies ever experience a B_{12} deficiency.

Other vitamin deficiencies

You may read that puppies need vitamins E and K. They do, but only when very young. By the time the pup is six weeks old he no longer needs them, or if he does, he finds K in his food and makes his own E as he does his C.

Unsaturated fatty acids, sometimes grouped as vitamin F, are required, but almost no diet is without them. Wheat-germ oil is sometimes fed to supply them, but since one drop of linseed oil a day furnishes plenty, they can be supplied in that way if needed.

Most of the meal-type foods contain considerable percentages of wheat germ, which carries all the unsaturated fatty acids any puppy could need.

Iron deficiency

Milk contains almost no iron. Puppies are born with enough iron to last them for several weeks, and if they are not plagued by the blood-draining activities of hookworms, they generally live on this original supply until they get their first solid food.

Meat, fresh and dry, has more than sufficient iron. There is no need to give more, if puppies are fed any meat, and all of the meal-type foods contain a great deal of iron.

If your pup has hookworms or has had a hemorrhage, you may need to give him iron, medicinally, to bring up his blood iron and make him want to eat. Your veterinarian can give you a sweet tonic with quickly available iron. If the pup will eat, he'll get enough iron from his food.

Salt deficiency

Strangely enough, most puppies need more salt than they get. Milk has inadequate amounts and, as in the case of iron, anything which causes a loss of blood reduces the sodium chloride to too low a level. A puppy does well on ½ to 1 percent salt level in his diet. Simply shaking a little iodized salt over the pup's food will help him greatly if he has a deficiency.

Other mineral deficiencies

Copper, cobalt, iodine, magnesium, potassium, and many other minerals are necessary to the health of all puppies, but it is hard to find any diet without sufficient quantities, and you may rest assured that all of the best commercial dog foods contain enough minerals for your puppy's needs.

PART TWO

PARASITES

Parasites are a special consideration and should be considered together, for in some instances they go hand in hand—fleas and tapeworms; mosquitoes and heartworms. Even certain drugs remove some species and not others.

It is important that you understand something about the common parasites. If you do, you won't go to your veterinarian and ask for "shots" for worms. You won't tell him, "But, Doctor, you dewormed this puppy six months ago; how could he have worms now?" You won't return from two weeks' summer vacation and be greeted by thousands of fleas which jump on your legs as you walk through the rooms, crawl on your clothes, and make you itch. You'll know how such an occurrence is possible, and even though it occurs in thousands of American homes every summer, you'll make sure that it can't happen in your home.

EXTERNAL PARASITES

Fleas

Fleas, unlike lice, do not develop on the dog, and for this reason your puppy is not very likely to pick up fleas from another dog. The adult fleas ride around on the dog, mating and laying eggs, while they eat to their hearts' content. The female fleas, when full of eggs, can be recognized by their huge brownish abdomens, which make them look very different from the lithe and graceful high-jumping males. The female fleas lay their eggs and rely on the travels of the dog to scatter them. Although you keep your dog as free of fleas as you yourself are, your premises may become infested with flea eggs. A neighbor's flea-covered dog may stay around your house and yard, leaving thousands of flea eggs behind him.

If your puppy or dog has fleas and you keep him in the house, you can be sure he will leave eggs all over the place. There they will stay as long as it is dry and cold, but let a nice, damp, warm spell of weather come in early summer and those eggs hatch out. Each occupant emerges as a tiny worm, eats organic matter, and grows until it is quite visible. Just before it pupates, it may be seen as a little brown and black worm, slightly more than an eighth of an inch long, moving about in cracks in the floor or maybe even in the tufts of your best overstuffed chair.

The worms spin cocoons and stay in them for several days.

Then they emerge as fleas, just as butterflies come from cocoons spun by caterpillars. At this stage the male and female fleas look alike, and both can jump prodigious distances. They climb on anything upright and jump for the first thing that goes past—a lady's calf or the pup. Fleas sometimes produce little raw spots on dogs where skin disease can find a place of access.

Symptoms of Infestation. The most obvious symptom of flea infestation, and one you are not likely to miss, is scratching. It would be hard for you to remain unaware of the presence of fleas on your puppy for very long anyway; they are perfectly visible, and a careful examination of the puppy's coat is enough to reveal the little pests.

Treatment. You can easily control fleas by using good flea powders, by dipping your puppy in rotenone solutions, by using a rinse after his bath, by using an insect-destroying foam, by spraying with an aerosol preparation or using sprays applied in other ways.

The latest discovery to control fleas, or insects of any kind, is called Vapona. It is available impregnated into dog collars and sold in all pet shops. It is also available in bars of resin that can be hung above a puppy or dog, or in a kennel, and the vapor given off destroys bugs. One bar effectively treats a room of 1000 cubic feet, killing the fleas both on and off the dog. It lasts about three months.

Lice

A louse lays its eggs (nits) and sticks them to the hair of the dog or puppy. The eggs hatch, and the little lice go to the skin to stay put or move around sluggishly, depending on whether they are the sucking or biting variety. You can find them nearly everywhere on the young puppy, but on older dogs they tend to like the ears best, especially those of long-haired dogs. Many think that dogs pick up the lice from their premises and that the lice can live for long periods off the dog, but it is more likely that they live no more than three days off their hosts.

Symptoms of Infestation. Puppies infested with lice soon take on an untidy appearance and gradually develop a stiff look. If your puppy looks this way, make a careful examination of his skin and hair to make sure that the presence of lice is the cause of his unthriftiness. It is amazing how many people own infested puppies and fail to discover the cause of their unhealthy condition. Even experienced kennel men may not recognize an infestation of lice. A large number of lice will make a puppy exceedingly anemic and cause death early in life. A badly infested puppy may even need a blood transfusion to survive.

Treatment. Inspect the puppy carefully for nits and remove any lice present by powdering him with a harmless potent louse powder, dipping him in the liquid preparation or in general using the same preparations available for fleas. But use them more thoroughly, because every inch of the pup must be covered. Repeat every ten or eleven days to kill lice that hatch from the nits.

Ticks

In some sections of the world, ticks are a very serious problem, but they are rare in young puppies unless the house in which the puppy is kept is infested. For this reason we shall not take the time to discuss the life history of ticks.

Most dogs become infested by running outside in brushy country. The insects can be eliminated by dips made for the purpose or simply by being pulled out of the dog's skin with tweezers. Be sure to pull the head out if possible. If ticks are a scourge, use tick powders, available in any drugstore.

Mange mites

Sarcoptic Mange. This is the form of mange that is caused by a roundish parasite, too small to be seen without magnification, which bores or tunnels through the skin. The disease spreads to human skin and back to animals.

Sarcoptic mange may appear anywhere on the puppy's body. Small points of infection appear as red spots somewhat raised, like little mounds. These spread and become continuous with the next until the skin shows large areas of reddish, thickened skin. Constant scratching inflames the area so that the combination of internal and external irritation leaves the skin in a pitiful condition. There is often some moisture if the inflammation is very severe.

Your veterinarian can give you medicine that will quickly eradicate sarcoptic mange from your puppy, but be sure that you yourself are not infested and spreading the parasite to the dog. There is no disgrace in getting any kind of parasite; the disgrace is in keeping it. If you have a skin condition resembling mange, and you know your puppy has sarcoptic mange, tell your doctor about it. The information will help both him and you, as it may make it unnecessary to do a painful scraping from one of the affected areas.

Demodectic Mange. Often called *red mange* or follicular mange, this is a skin affliction which used to be considered incurable. With the discovery of the effectiveness of rotenone and other drugs, it is now among the simplest of skin diseases to cure, but it is an insidious disease because while you are curing one area another is developing under the hair.

The cigar-shaped mite gets into the hair follicle and reproduces there, and the young mites spread to other follicles. They are so small and require so much time to reproduce and grow that many weeks may pass before they show on the dog's skin. When they do show, the first indication is a spot of thinned hair, not entirely bald. This usually occurs on the face, somewhere around the eyes, or on the front legs. There are, of course, exceptions, but certainly 75 percent of all cases show up first in these areas. There is no serious escape of fluid, but just a harmless-looking baldish spot. This spot may be soon cured with medicine which your veterinarian will give you, but meanwhile incubation is proceeding in many other spots on your puppy. The next thing you know, there are a dozen larger areas where the hair is sparser than usual.

Dogs are often brought to our clinic with nine tenths of their bodies denuded of hair, but they are curable even in such a condition. It takes some time to do it, and usually a month elapses before the hair returns. If your puppy has suffered from demodectic mange, you must keep everlastingly on the watch for the reappearance of new spots and treat them early.

WORMS AND OTHER INTERNAL PARASITES

Roundworms

While not so severe in their effects as some parasites that puppies harbor, roundworms do untold damage in the aggregate. They account annually for the deaths of thousands of puppies. The puppies die not only because the worms are in the stomach and intestines but also because of lung infestation that leads to pneumonia. How does this situation come about?

The puppy gets the roundworm egg in its mouth. The egg may be ingested from the mother's teats, fur, or feet. Or it may be picked up from the bone that the mother dragged around in her run and brought into the puppy box. Or it may be picked up directly by mouth from the ground or possibly be blown in dust onto food which the pup then eats. After the egg reaches his mouth, here is what happens:

It is swallowed. It has a tough coat or shell, so resistant that it will live in the soil for years and stand soaking in some disinfectants; but when the acids of the stomach attack it, the shell is dissolved, and the little worm within the shell is liberated. In this form it is the larva. The tiny, microscopic thing is moved into the intestine, and at once it bores through the intestinal lining until it gets into the blood or lymph, by which route it enters the general circulation.

Then the larva floats about in the blood stream until, after further development, it ends up in the lungs. There it bores through into the air passages and produces the cough characteristic of heavy infestation. One lonesome larva probably would have little effect, but large numbers of them cause great irritation and often pneumonia, as they damage the lungs. The larva is finally gagged up into the throat and is promptly swallowed. It grows to adulthood, attaining a length of about four inches, and lives in the stomach or intestine the rest of its life, migrating up and down so as not to be too close to other roundworms, except at mating time.

When mating time arrives, the male and female copulate. The fertilized female lays great numbers of eggs, which are passed out of the puppy with the feces and, if not cleaned up, may become scattered and infest the premises. Rain is actually helpful in scattering feces and washing the eggs into the ground. Here they incubate for considerable time, the period depending upon the temperature and amount of humidity.

There, in a nutshell, is the life history of the roundworm. There are two general kinds that may infest your puppy, but both have more or less similar life histories. Both are characteristically parasites of puppies and young dogs. As dogs get older they seem to develop a partial immunity to roundworms, so that fewer roundworm eggs are found in the feces of adult dogs.

Symptoms of Infestation. If your puppy is heavily infested with this common worm, he will probably have a cough and may perhaps even cough up worms which you can see. His condition will become unhealthy, and he will give every evidence of having some ailment, perhaps even verminous pneumonia. If the infestation is a light one, you may have trouble detecting it and fail to do so altogether. However, a fecal examination made by a competent veterinarian will disclose the presence of roundworm eggs, and you will be able to treat your puppy for this specific type of worm if necessary.

Treatment. There are many de-worming drugs available. The simplest and most efficient is piperazine which your pet's doctor can provide, or which you can obtain in any store where pet home remedies are sold. There is another product containing the same drug which is impregnated into flea collars and destroys roundworms, hookworms, and whipworms. It is available only through veterinarians under the name of Task. Like piperazine, it can be mixed with food.

Hookworms

In some respects the life cycle of the hookworm and that of the roundworm are similar. This is principally due to the fact that both spend part of their embryonic stage in the blood.

Hookworms are not harmful as eggs because the eggs are not infestive. After the eggs appear in the puppy's stool they hatch, provided the temperature and moisture are both favorable for their development, and the larval form goes through five pupations before it finally is infestive—approximately two weeks. Then it is usually ingested, although it is believed to be able to bore through the skin of the toes. When it reaches the intestine it works itself through the intestinal lining and becomes a blood parasite.

By whatever way it gains admission to the blood, it finally arrives at the lungs, is coughed up and swallowed, and attaches itself to the intestinal lining by the hooks of its mouth (these hooks are responsible for its name). It lives by sucking blood. One hookworm can draw about a thimbleful of blood from a puppy in one week, so you can see why very early recognition is imperative if you are to save your infested puppy.

Symptoms of Infestation. Hookworms are dangerous to both young puppies and mature dogs alike because of the anemia they produce. Sometimes hundreds of these parasites will cling to an animal's intestine, sucking blood all the time and secreting toxin. If your puppy is suffering from a hookworm infestation, his body tissue will be pale. You can see this pallor in the gums, the normally red areas around the eyes, et cetera. He will also have a general loss of condition. A fecal examination will disclose the presence of hookworm eggs and indicate the severity of infestation.

Treatment. Let your veterinarian prescribe. He may inject your pup to quickly eliminate hookworms, or supply you with Task for you to put in its food.

Whipworms

This little parasite is about half an inch long in its body part but has a long protrusion or flagellum from its front end that gives it the appearance of a whip. The flagellum is about an inch and a half long and is sewed into the puppy's intestinal lining to act as a means of anchorage. A favorite place for the whipworm to settle down is the cecum, a blind gut arrangement located at the upper end of the large intestine. There was a time when whipworms presented a problem in elimination and operations were performed to remove the infested dog's cecum, but this is never necessary any more.

The whipworm egg is believed to require twenty days for incubation at optimum conditions. Like the roundworm egg, it is resistant. Once it is ingested and its shell removed, the little larvae are believed to become attached to the intestine without spending any time in the blood of the dog.

Puppies rarely harbor whipworms in the first few weeks of life.

Symptoms of Infestation. Whipworms produce a toxin or poison that causes a loss of condition in the puppy. Large numbers of these parasites can damage the intestinal lining to some extent. There is considerable absorption of fluid from the cecum, and when many whipworms are located in it the puppy acts poisoned.

A whipworm-infested puppy often becomes anemic, loses his appetite, becomes stiff, and is no longer interested in play. His woebegone expression indicates the urgency of the need for a fecal examination.

Treatment. There are now several remedies effective against whipworms. Get one from your pet's doctor. He may supply Task, especially if he finds the pup has other forms of worms.

Tapeworms

The tapeworm most commonly found in young puppies is the type whose intermediate host is the dog flea. The second most common one is that which has the rabbit as its intermediate host, and a puppy must eat part of a raw rabbit to become infested.

The flea-host type's life history is as follows: The puppy eats a flea in whose body is a tapeworm head enclosed in a cyst. When the flea is partially digested, the tapeworm head is liberated. It adheres to the intestinal lining by suckers and re-

mains there throughout its life. This microscopic head section
grows, and from it an extension develops. On the tail of this
extension another is added. To this another is added, and so
on, the worm becoming longer and longer. Each addition,
known as a segment, or proglottid, puts a strain on the segments above it. When the worm is finally developed, the segments closest to the head have been pulled out by the strain
of the others until they look like a long thread. Naturally, the
closer the segments are to the tail end, the fatter they are.

These last segments become filled with eggs after the tapeworm has mated. It is interesting to note that one segment on
the same worm may be male and another female, so that the
worm can mate with itself by twisting around and letting the
lower segments touch those higher up.

The segments at the end, with their ripened eggs—which,
when seen through a microscope, appear like bunches of
grapes surrounded by a thin envelope—drop off. They may be
found crawling out of the puppy's anus, on his bed, or sometimes clinging to the hair under his tail, dried and resembling
small grains of brown rice.

The larval form of the flea—a worm—feeds on these segments and finds much nourishment in them. In consuming the
meat of the segment, the larva ingests the eggs, which, as we
have seen, become cysts in their bodies. Then the flea larva
spins a cocoon, where it pupates, and from its cocoon emerges
a little flea, containing within its body the head of a tapeworm.
The fleas crawl into the mouths of puppies or grown dogs, and
the cycle starts all over again.

In less than three weeks after an infested flea is swallowed
by your puppy you can find tapeworm segments on or in the
stools of that puppy. These segments hold the eggs well, and
it is exceptional to find eggs from the flea-host tapeworm in a
dog's stool unless one of the segments happens to be mashed.

Diagnosis can be easily made by seeing the segments on the stool or around the anus.

The rabbit-host tapeworm has a different life history. A dog with the worms in his intestine defecates where there is grass. Some of the eggs from the tapeworm (this type lays eggs) stick to the grass, and the blades grow up carrying the eggs with them. A rabbit eats the grass and, of course, the eggs along with it. The egg contains the larval form which, unlike the flea-host worm larva, gets into the blood and eventually winds up in the liver as a favorite spot. Here the rabbit's body forms a cyst about it, and it lives within the cyst until the rabbit is shot, skinned, and its liver fed by an unsuspecting hunter to his puppy. The liver is digested, but not the worm. The worm promptly attaches itself to the intestine and grows many segments, each somewhat fatter and larger than those of the flea-host tapeworm.

Then the eggs are laid and pass out in the feces. Segments of the worm also drop off, where they are often seen in the stool. The presence of these worms may be determined both by the segments on the stool and by eggs in the stool, which may be found with a microscope.

Symptoms of Infestation. You have perhaps been told that the presence of a tapeworm, in either dogs or humans, causes a great increase in appetite. You will not find this to be necessarily true, particularly in puppies. Chances are that the infested puppy's appetite will decrease rather than increase, and he may get the swollen, potbellied appearance characteristic of malnourished and unthrifty animals. If he has many tapeworms, you will almost always find segments in his stool or on him or his bedding, so that diagnosis is an easy matter. A fecal examination may not reveal eggs of the flea-host tapeworm because, as stated, they are firmly contained within the segments.

Treatment. Your veterinarian may give you arecoline with instructions on how to use it. Or Nemural or Teneathane or perhaps a newer drug. If the full dose is given at one time, it may cause nausea and vomiting. In that case arecoline can be given in split doses, one third every seven minutes. The drug is cumulative, and within a half hour the worms may all be discharged.

Coccidia

These minute organisms, great killers of puppies, are too often overlooked as a cause of disease. Their effects often make the puppy's owner sure his pup has "distemper." And when the disease does not kill, it weakens and makes housebreaking almost impossible. Yet most puppies have the disease at some time in their lives, so don't be surprised if your puppy has his bout with it. The organisms, or coccidia, are so small that they are almost in a class with bacteria.

The puppy becomes infected by getting some of these coccidia into his mouth. As soon as they are ingested they begin to go through a cycle of form changes. At one stage they are able to bore through into the cells lining the intestine. There they multiply in enormous quantities, doing damage directly proportional to their numbers. The infective form of the organism is then spewed out into the intestine and passed out in the stool. Your veterinarian can look at a sample of stool with his microscope and diagnose the presence of coccidia without guesswork.

Symptoms. The symptoms of coccidia are almost the same as those most people associate with distemper. About the only difference is that puppies do not shun light as they do in Carré's disease. The eyes fill with pus, the nose discharges, the temperature often goes to 104 degrees F., and the stools are fluid.

Treatment. Probably more medicines have been reported as cures for coccidiosis than for any other known disease. The cure notices continue to be circulated, but so far the truth seems to be that no known drug cures the disease in dogs. It improves of its own accord.

The body slowly builds up immunity over a period of about three to four weeks. At the end of this time the puppy is immune for life, but only against that specific form of coccidiosis which he had. He can and often does have two forms at the same time, or one after another.

Medical treatment is merely palliative. The diarrhea can be lessened by drugs prescribed by your veterinarian. Diet is most important, provided your patient will eat. A diet without fat has proven disastrous. Diets containing 20 percent fat seem just right. In one study twenty-two puppies were infected purposely. They were fed 25 percent fat, which slows digestion, and adequate proteins. Every pup continued to gain almost as though he had not been sick.

Heartworms

In many sections of the world, especially where mosquitoes are prevalent, puppies become infested with heartworms. These are eight-inch-long, thin, whitish parasites that live in the heart, often in such numbers as to seriously interfere with blood circulation. They give birth to live larvae, microscopic in size, which live in the blood until a mosquito, in sucking blood from an infested dog, takes them into its system. There they undergo a change, and when the mosquito attacks another dog they are transmitted to that dog's blood. Then they are able to grow. They remain in the heart and in turn give birth to more larvae. Sucking lice, especially, help to increase the number of heartworms in a puppy.

Symptoms. A puppy won't show evidence of heartworms,

even though he was infected while quite young, until he is nearly grown. The chief sign is the inability to stand any prolonged exercise without playing out. If your puppy should show such a sign, look at his gums and tongue; they will be quite purple. Of course anemic pups play out easily, too, but from other causes, such as hookworms.

Another symptom is coughing whenever any pull is exerted on a leash attached to a collar or when your puppy pulls against his chain if he is tied out. There are also many other causes for such coughing.

Your veterinarian should be consulted. He will take a few drops of the puppy's blood and study it for heartworm larvae.

Treatment. Leave the cure to your puppy's doctor. He may prescribe pills to be given frequently over a period of weeks or he may prefer to give injections of an antimony drug.

Prevention. There is no way to immunize pups against heartworm. If you live in a heartworm section, you must keep him in a screened kennel or indoors, especially at night; keep him where mosquitoes cannot reach him, and keep him free from fleas and lice.

Because mosquitoes mostly fly at night, a Vapona bar hung in the kennel will kill the pests that manage to get inside, before they have a chance to sting the puppy.

Trichinosis

Feeding raw or undercooked pork to a dog has the same consequences as serving it to human beings; the danger of trichinosis is the same to both. Encysted in their tiny capsules in the flesh of a large proportion of swine—especially of the garbage-fed—are thousands of tiny worms. If they enter the stomach of your puppy, each eventually multiples, and tunnel about until they come to rest and make cysts of their own. And this naturally affects the host, which is your puppy.

Symptoms. Trichina love to settle down in the big breathing muscle—the diaphragm—which separates the chest cavity from the abdomen. This invasion naturally produces pain and stiffness. Every movement of any infested muscle is painful.

Severe symptoms cause groaning from the pain of movement.

And, worst of all, there is no treatment. You must wait for the puppy to get used to the parasites, and this requires a period of nearly two months.

PART THREE

PUPPIES AND YOUR HEALTH

Many persons are uncertain whether bringing a puppy into the home will increase the chances of illness in the family. Dog owners frequently wonder if their dogs have caused illness in the house.

I can tell you that specific instances of human beings contracting diseases from dogs are so rare that they make news. But it is interesting to know what these instances actually are.

The most common is ringworm. Any pet, dog or cat, with this skin ailment is a potential threat to the family. If your puppy contracts it, have him treated completely and tell the family "hands off" until he is cured.

Another trouble is sarcoptic mange. Skin specialists who find it on persons often ask if you have a pet? Does the animal itch? Has it any bare spots? If so, have it promptly cured.

One dangerous disease that dogs can transmit to humans is canicola fever. This produces heart and kidney damage if untreated. Now we can protect our dogs against it, and in my estimation, anyone who does not have his puppy protected is remiss.

Babies playing in sandboxes where fleas from dogs may hatch have sometimes swallowed the fleas and gotten tapeworms. This is a good reason for keeping every pup and dog both tapeworm-free and flea-free. Then there have been a few rare cases of babies having in some way taken roundworm eggs from dog droppings into their mouths. The eggs hatch, and the larvae travel about in the blood and have been known to end up in the eyes causing blindness.

All of the above are really rare, but the knowledge helps us avoid such possibilities in our families.

PART FOUR

FIRST AID AND MEDICINES

Adequate care and intelligent handling are usually sufficient to keep a puppy in good health. But even a healthy animal, like a healthy child, cannot be perfectly guarded against every eventuality. Accidents do happen; emergencies arise in spite of every precaution. The most conscientious owner cannot know when his puppy will surprise a porcupine on a particular country path; he cannot prevent his dog from killing and eating a poisoned rabbit that wanders across his back yard.

Two things the owner can do. By exercising reasonable and humane precautions, he can avoid the accidents resulting from carelessness. He can learn how to cope with emergencies when they do arise.

Every year thousands of pets are lost needlessly simply because their owners have never taken the time to familiarize themselves with a few simple principles of first-aid and emergency treatment. The owner who has never learned how to handle the common emergency situations becomes panicky and does nothing to help his injured pet—or does worse than nothing, the wrong thing. The person who has no understanding of the normal recuperative processes or powers of animals too quickly assumes that the best he can do for an animal that has been hurt is to put it out of the reach of pain and so destroys his pet when it might have recovered easily and completely.

Too many puppy owners feel that since they prefer to have their veterinarian prescribe for all serious pet problems there is no necessity for them to be able to handle difficult or unpleasant situations themselves. Such owners should remember, however, that emergencies have a way of happening at inconvenient moments. Even in metropolitan areas there are often times when a veterinarian is not immediately available, and in most sections of the country it may well take several hours to reach a veterinarian when he is needed. So long as that is true, the owner who doesn't take the trouble to find out what he can do to help his pup in an emergency is risking the animal's life foolishly.

Any owner can be and should be prepared to administer first aid to an injured pet. He should know how to restrain a puppy that is frightened or in pain, so that it will not harm itself or others. He should know how to stop the flow of blood from a wound, how to relieve the pain as much as possible, how to protect the pet until the veterinarian reaches it. He should know what not to do. The skills and techniques are not difficult to learn or to apply. They are available to everyone— the cheapest and best insurance a person can get against the loss of his pet.

RESTRAINT AND FIRST AID

Before you can attempt any sort of treatment for an injured puppy you must know how to protect yourself and how to prevent the patient from doing damage to himself or escaping before you have taken care of him properly. Restraint of some sort is usually necessary to administer first aid and always necessary when surgery of any sort is involved.

Your pup's defenses consist of biting and clawing. Unless his nails have been kept trimmed, they may be almost as sharp as cat's claws, and his little teeth, before the new ones come in, are as sharp as needles. He must be held so that he cannot reach the handler. His head must be covered or his mouth must be tied closed. An injured pet is often a panic-stricken animal. Under such circumstances even the most gentle animal may bite and scratch when you attempt to help him. Don't blame him, and don't destroy him as vicious. Remember that biting in a normal reaction of a frightened or injured animal. Remember, too, that his pain may have subsided for the moment and that in handling him you may have caused it to recur with terrible intensity. Don't expect the puppy to respond as he usually does. Expect him to act like what he is—an animal in pain.

What can you do when you see a pup that has been struck by a car lying in the street, probably surrounded by a crowd of sympathetic but helpless people? For one thing, you can move him out of the street. He has dragged himself ten feet. He can move his tail, so you know his back is not broken. His pelvis has probably been crushed. Approach the pup from the side, with his head at your left. Put a hand near his head. If he makes no attempt to bite, with your left hand grasp as large a handful of loose skin as possible, high up on the neck, and hold tight. So long as you hold fast he can't bite, because he can neither shake himself loose nor turn his head far enough to reach you.

The pup can be lifted by this grip until he is high enough so that your right hand can reach under his chest just between the front legs, thus encircling the body. The puppy will not try to bite your clothing. He cannot reach your hand. He is held too low to be able to bite your face. Let us suppose you want to carry him into your home to his bed, or that you want to put him into your automobile. Just push your right arm forward and place him gently where he will rest, pulling your hand backward from under him as he reclines.

But suppose that the pup, when you put a hand near him, snaps at it. Or suppose when you start to lift him he screams. This attracts people, perhaps gives them the impression you are being cruel. What then? This is when a simple piece of cloth, three feet long and three or four inches wide, does the trick. Cross the ends and start to tie a knot, but instead of drawing it taut, let a loop hang down while you hold an end of the cloth in each hand. The dog is now approached from the front. Your hands are far enough apart so that he cannot reach either one. Slip the loose loop over his nose, about one and a half inches from the tip, draw it tight, tie a knot under his chin, and then bring both ends around his neck, tying them in a bowknot behind his ears. When you have done this you can safely lift him as described above.

But suppose again that he is badly lacerated about the face and chest, and savage. It would be cruel to place a tie around his muzzle. What can you do then? Obtain a blanket and spread it on the ground beside him. Then make a slip lasso, toss it around his neck, and drag him gently onto the blanket so that two people can pull the four corners taut, and in this way make a stretcher of it.

The blanket may be used in another way: fold it to the

smallest size that will cover the pup's chest and head, with
enough extra to extend several inches in front of his nose. This
will probably be eight thicknesses, and even if a large puppy
should bite through it, he can inflict very little damage. The
folded blanket is dropped squarely over his head and shoulders, and he is grasped firmly from behind, with one hand in
back of each shoulder. With this grip the pup can be lifted
with the blanket wrapped around him and held securely in
front of the handler.

When the injured puppy is safely in the car or in the home,
he may be restrained by the mouth tie for examination of
broken bones, gashes, bruises, internal bleeding, or any other
injuries that may be indicated.

Suppose you are handling a pup dazed from a head injury
inflicted by a glancing blow of an automobile bumper. You
have cornered him, tied his mouth, and started to carry him.
Everything goes well until he wriggles out of your grip. Then
you remember that you neglected to snap a leash to his collar.
When you have caught the pup and fastened the leash, remember to take the time to tighten his collar. In his struggling he
will probably slip the collar over his head unless it is drawn
tighter than usual.

If he won't be led, run the leash backward, encircle his
chest behind his front legs, and loop the leash through as if he
were in a giant knot. You can then pull forward with a lifting
force. It will usually make him walk, even when he is not
leash-broken. By grasping the surcingle just above the puppy's
back, you can move him along almost as you would carry a
suitcase.

Principles of first aid

The principles of first aid that the puppy owner needs to
master are simple and relatively few, but they are of vital im-

portance in handling emergencies. Whether an animal that has been injured is to recover quickly or slowly, whether it is to be completely restored or marked or scarred—indeed, whether the animal is to survive at all—often depends upon the treatment it gets immediately after it is hurt. The following paragraphs are intended to give the general information you need and at the same time provide you with a reference manual in which you may quickly find the specific way to handle any emergency that may arise in connection with your pet.

Shock

Any severe injury—a burn, a struggle, a fight, or even a severe fright—may bring on this condition. The puppy usually seems to be prostrated in a semi-oblivious state, yet apparently anxious. The nervous system is in depression, sometimes so severe as to cause complete immobility. On the other hand, an occasional puppy may suffer the opposite effect, so that it seems to be in a state of nervous excitement. The pulse is slow and weak, the breathing shallow. Often, as the animal recovers, the pulse becomes too rapid, and the temperature may rise well above normal.

First aid consists in covering the pup so his temperature will rise to normal. High artificial heat is not necessary if the animal is at home in familiar surroundings. Administer a stimulant, such as coffee, then let him rest. Occasional fondling is often reassuring and helpful. Recovery may take an hour to several hours.

Heat stroke

Fat dogs are the most frequent victims of heat strokes.

We are all conscious of the refreshing sensation of a breeze in hot weather. This is due to evaporation of moisture from our bodies and the consequent cooling of the surface of the body. The bodies of animals are cooled by the same process, which is aided by evaporation in the throat and mouth when the pet becomes overheated and pants. Dogs have few sweat glands in the skin compared to humans and horses, but they do have some. When an animal is sufficiently cooled by bodily evaporation, he stops panting.

Panting, in itself, is a normal method of reducing body temperature. It may sometimes be an indication of thirst. A hot, panting pup is obviously evaporating an abnormal amount of moisture from his body and needs to replenish the loss.

In a heat stroke, however, the panting is sharp and continuous. The puppy seems to be "burning up," his tongue turns purple, and he finds it difficult to catch his breath. You know he has been exposed to great heat, possibly to excitement. What should you do until the veterinarian arrives?

Remember the principle of cooling we have just discussed: the evaporation of water reduces body temperature. Lay the pup on a flat surface and pour cold water over him until he is thoroughly soaked. Set up an electric fan a few feet away, turn its blast directly on him, and keep on adding water as it evaporates. Take the pup's temperature occasionally. Usually his fever will drop in less than half an hour from about 108 to 101 degrees. When it has come down to normal or nearly so, dry the dog with a towel, and keep him out of the heat.

If an electric fan is not available, a cold-water enema is advisable. If this is impossible, immersion in cold water is a satisfactory method of reducing the temperature quickly. A great many puppies have been saved in this manner.

Puppies are frequently afflicted by heat stroke in cars. If this should happen, stop for water and lay your patient on the floor in front. As soon as you have got the water, drive on with the cowl ventilator open, so that the draft will blow directly on him. Pour on the water, keeping him wet, and before many miles his temperature will have dropped to normal.

Anyone who takes a pup on a long trip in very hot weather should be aware of the danger of a heat stroke and be careful to avoid it. He should carry a pan and water for the pet. The animal that is losing an unusual amount of water by evaporation needs to replace it by drinking frequently. If he has enough water, he is much less likely to succumb to the heat.

Accidents

The most common cause of accidents among pets is the automobile. It is so common that companies that insure dogs' lives often exempt death by automobile from policies. Pups will dash across the street to get to another dog. Even those which are so well trained that they will wait for a car to pass will walk across the street behind it only to be struck by a car coming the opposite way. The brightest have not learned to look both ways, to anticipate so far into the future.

When a puppy is struck by an automobile, you must first restrain him (see page 135) and then treat him for shock. Look at his gums to see if he is losing blood too rapidly. If his gums appear gray or white, he probably has suffered an organic injury and is bleeding internally. Roll up long strips of bandage—an old sheet may be torn in strips for the purpose. Have an assistant stretch the pet out and hold his front and hind legs. Then wrap the bandage around his body tightly, corset-fashion. Keep on wrapping it until you have made a good firm support. Be sure that it will not pull together in a narrow roll around his abdomen when he moves. It must form a long tube, which holds the animal's organs relatively immobile, so that a clot can form and remain in place. Without this firmness and pressure, the organs can move freely and break the blood clot loose. Do all you can to keep the puppy quiet. The veterinarian, when he comes, will administer a drug to check bleeding and may decide upon a transfusion if he feels that the transfused blood will not run into the abdomen and be wasted. Whatever you do, do not move him far after an accident if there are indications of internal bleeding. He can bleed to death very quickly. He may be saved if you keep him quiet.

If a puppy does bleed internally, what becomes of the blood that runs into the abdomen? When a clot forms it is composed of red and white cells, plasma, and fibrinogen, which causes coagulation. As it forms, the clot squeezes out a fluid or serum. This serum can be, and is, soaked up by the peritoneum (the lining of the abdomen and covering of the organs). Obviously the serum gets back into the circulation and thus helps to increase the blood volume. Many of the red cells which transport oxygen through the body are in the clot. This clot does not persist permanently as a liverlike lump. Instead a process called lysis occurs. The cells simply dissolve into the fluid in the abdomen. Their covering disintegrates and releases the contents. The fluid is now circulated, but only a small amount is utilized by the body; most of it, including the red pigment, is passed out of the body through the urine as waste. When you see your weak but mending patient urinating what appears to be blood, don't presume he is passing blood from his kidneys and bladder; it is probably blood-coloring matter. Indeed, anticipate his doing this. This fact is sometimes used as a diagnostic means of demonstrating internal hemorrhage which occurred several days before the red color is seen.

Cuts

Pups hustling through barbed-wire fences, stepping on broken bottles, scratching in ash piles, and stepping on concealed metal scraps come home gashed, bleeding, and torn. They seldom bleed to death.

Most of the cuts that occur on animal skins are triangular tears. Some, of course, are clean, straight cuts. In either case only a limited kind of first aid should be administered. In animal saliva there is an enzyme that digests germs. The surface of a puppy's tongue is made up of small, tough scales so strong that he can wear flesh away if he wants to. There is no better way of cleaning a cut than allowing him to do it. He will lick away all dead flesh or debris and kill germs as he does so. He will heal his own wounds.

First aid consists not of strapping the cut together with adhesive tape, nor of binding up the wound, unless it is bleeding badly, but of allowing the patient to clean his wounds and then having the veterinarian treat them. So there need be no hurry to rush your pet to the doctor; take the puppy within a few hours. When you do, the veterinarian will cut away any dead edges on the flap and suture it in place, so that when it has healed no ugly scar will remain.

However, there are cuts that pups cannot reach to lick. In long-haired dogs these cuts may be covered with hair, which should be trimmed off about the area. Or they may be on parts of the body, such as the neck, head, face, and shoulders, which the dog cannot reach. In such a case, clean the cuts yourself (peroxide is excellent for this purpose), and take him to the hospital as soon as possible.

Cuts deep in the feet usually cause profuse bleeding, since this area is filled with blood vessels. A cut of this sort should always be examined to see if a long sliver has remained in it. After this examination it is necessary to stop the bleeding. A plug of cotton pressed against the opening and a pressure bandage which holds it there will quickly check the bleeding. If the cut should hemorrhage, apply a tourniquet immediately

above or below the wrist joint. It must be loosened and re-
applied every ten minutes. On the trip to the veterinarian take
along some cloths to absorb blood which may stain the car or
clothes.

The most dangerous cuts are those made by filthy objects.
These cuts may heal or mat over with hair which becomes
part of a scab, and tetanus (lockjaw) germs frequently infect
such wounds. Since they can develop only in a cut or puncture
wound which the air cannot reach, cuts of this sort must be
opened, cleansed, and kept open until they have been disin-
fected and sutured. There are some wounds that are best left
unsutured for a considerable length of time. These must be
flushed daily while they heal from the bottom out, and they
are sutured to avoid unsightly scars only when the healing
process has reached the surface layers of the skin.

Animal bites and poisonous snake or insect bites need very
different treatment, so we shall consider them separately.

Bites

Animal Bites. It is sometimes important to determine the
kind of bite to be treated. The bite of a dog, cat, and even that
of a rat, can usually be distinguished by the number of teeth
marks. Mature dogs seldom bite growing puppies. The pup,
when attacked, scratches, tucks his tail between his legs, or
runs cowering away—signals to the grown dog to let the pup
alone.

Cat Bites. These often become seriously infected on puppies. The skin should not be allowed to heal quickly over
them. First aid often consists in hurrying the animal to the
doctor. If infected, the punctures become large abscesses which
burst, carrying with them large areas of skin which have been
killed in the process of abscess formation. A bite that has
been allowed to abscess takes much longer to heal than does

a properly treated bite, and the new skin which eventually covers the sore spot will never have hair.

Some bites result in jagged tears which may require suturing. If you know how, you may be able to do a good job, but whether you or your veterinarian does it, don't wait until the skin has shrunken.

Snake Bites. First aid in snake bites is extremely important. When you suspect a rapidly increasing swelling to be the result of a rattlesnake, copperhead, or water-moccasin bite, there is usually sufficient time to reach a veterinarian. If you can't reach him, try your family doctor. Many physicians have saved animal lives in emergencies. If neither a veterinarian nor a doctor is available, buy some potassium-permanganate solution, which a druggist will prepare for you. Make a deep X-shaped cut right over the fang marks, remembering that they are pushed in at an angle and not straight. This cut induces bleeding. Drop the potassium permanganate into the cut and hold it there for a moment. Apply a tourniquet above the bite if it is on the leg or foot. If the swelling ascends the leg and reaches the body, you may lose the animal.

Spider Bites. The only dangerous spider bites are those of the black widow. This spider has a predilection for old bones. Spiders are often found inside old skulls of horses and cattle that have died and been left unburied. Pups, too, enjoy such things, and so are often bitten by these poisonous insects. The bites are usually on the lips or face. Swelling occurs and increases proportionately with the amount of venom the spider injects. One bite may kill a pup, although it is unlikely. Very little can be done at home. If you know where the spider that bit your pet lives, a fine opportunity is offered to do some spraying and exterminate the spider and possibly all of her young, thus saving other pets and human beings from being bitten.

Foreign bodies

No first-aid discussion could be complete without suggestions as to the removal of foreign bodies.

In the Mouth. Pups sometimes overestimate their ability to manipulate certain bones. It is common to find such bones caught in various positions—wedged across the roof of the mouth between the back teeth; driven down into the gum beside a tooth; driven through the soft tissue below the lower jaw; stuck between two teeth; stuck on top of a molar tooth; or covering several teeth.

A T-bone from a lamb chop is sometimes caught across the pup's mouth between the back teeth, with its sharp point sticking into the throat. The puppy paws desperately at his mouth, and the owner often thinks that the end has surely come. Older pups sometimes chew two- or three-inch shank bones from lamb so that the rounded bone slips down over their teeth, and they can't close their mouths without forcing the sharp edges of the bone farther down against the gums. These dogs become frantic.

Many other kinds of foreign bodies become wedged in the teeth or stuck in the mouth. Any pup may have such accidents. The mouth must be opened and the object pulled out. Whenever possible, it is wise to rush the pet to the veterinarian, who has the instruments to remove the obstruction without difficulty.

In the Stomach. If you do not actually see a pup eat a foreign object, you can never be sure that the pup does have it in his stomach. You may have seen him eat gravel or sand, or chew on an old doll. But circumstantial evidence is usually all that is necessary. If a small item the dog was playing with is missing and the dog begins to show evidence of stomach pain, it is time for action.

Suppose you suspect that your puppy has swallowed one of your child's iron jacks, the crisscross gadget the child picks up when he bounces a ball. The pup will probably show some evidence of stomach pain, and you should act at once. Mix about an ounce of peroxide with an ounce of water and pour it down the dog's throat. Vomiting will occur very soon. When it begins, lift the pup by his back legs so that his forepaws are touching the ground and his head is down. In almost every case the jack will be regurgitated the first time.

You may be surprised sometime to pick up your pup and hear stones rattling together in his stomach. Actually you shouldn't be too astonished, for this is a fairly common occurrence. And it shouldn't worry you very much. Stones can always be recovered by the peroxide treatment. Puppies with gravel impactions in their stomachs can be relieved by the same means. Mineral oil should be given fifteen minutes after the peroxide, to help move along the gravel that has entered the intestine. Puppies which have overeaten on dog biscuits and have swallowed large pieces, sometimes cry with pain and may even have fits. Emptying their stomachs usually relieves pain and stops such fits.

Remedies of this sort for the removal of foreign bodies are properly classified as first aid. More difficult cases should be left to the veterinarian. With X-rays he can locate bullets, needles, pins, spark plugs, and any of the hundreds of other odd and dangerous objects that dogs have been known to swallow.

In the Rectum. If your pup squats, strains, cries, and possibly exudes a little blood from his anus, it is likely that he has a foreign body in the rectum. If a constipated mass is considered a foreign body, he surely has. Not infrequently the stoppage is caused by sharp bone splinters which were not properly softened and digested in his stomach. Poultry, pork, and lamb bones are the most likely to cause such difficulties. Since any movement of the sharp bones is extremely painful, the dog refrains from defecating. In time the fecal material piles up behind them and soon a solid, dry mass with sharp bones sticking out of it precludes all passage.

Puppies are notorious for eating their bedding or for chewing up cloth, leather, straw, hay, and all sorts of things that produce colonic impactions.

First aid consists of enemas to soften the mass, though they often are not sufficiently effective to allow passage of the material. Humane considerations indicate a prompt visit to the doctor, who will probably first soften the mass and then gently reach in with an instrument and crush it into small particles. Occasionally an oily enema is sufficiently lubricating to permit the stool to be passed without great difficulty or pain. In difficult cases the veterinarian may have to pull out the sharp pieces with his instrument to avoid cutting.

Needles are frequently found in the rectums of dogs. Often a thread hanging from the anus is a good indication of the cause of the pain. If the needle is just inside and can be felt, an ingenious person with a small wire cutter such as electricians use can snip the needle in half and remove the halves separately. Generally, however, this job is best left to the doctor, who will use anesthesia and a speculum to see clearly what he is doing.

In the Skin. Foreign bodies in puppies' skin or feet are usually splinters or bullets, although other objects, such as pitchfork tines, glass chips, and porcupine quills, are not as uncommon as most people think. Common sense dictates the quick removal of such objects, whenever possible, in order to relieve the animal. It also dictates the injection of an antiseptic into the wound. If a bullet has come to rest against a rib, and it can be seen through the hole, you should—for once—do what your first impulse tells you; pull it out with the family tweezers and cleanse the wound.

Children often put elastic bands around the neck, leg, tail, ear, or even the penis of their puppies. The hair covers the band and it goes unnoticed by adults until swelling starts. By that time it may have cut through the skin. There is little the owner himself can do after he has removed the band. If the skin gaps too wide, have the veterinarian suture it to prevent formation of a hairless scar. Ropes and small chains may also cut deeply through the tender skin. Most people have seen at least one animal with a hairless band of skin around the neck —mute evidence that some negligent owner left a rope or chain on until it cut the puppy's neck. Having callously injured the animal, he failed even to have the gaping skin sutured.

Porcupine Quillings. In many states in the United States, and in all parts of Canada, porcupines are common. To a puppy a porcupine is a curiosity needing to be investigated. He gets close to the prickly black creature who may be partially curled up to protect itself. Then wham! the porcupine's tail— its only aggressive weapon of protection—slaps against the puppy's anatomy, driving sharp, short black quills deeply into the muscle. The puppy cries out in pain, generally retreats and, likely as not, rolls on the quills and drives them in deeper. I have pulled thousands of quills from mature dogs which have attacked porcupines and removed the long white body quills as well as tail quills—but from puppies, only the tail quills. A quill, which is only a modified hair lighty attached to the porcupine's skin, has small reverse barbs protruding from the shaft for a quarter of an inch down from the sharp point. Under a microscope the barbs look like the prickles on a thistle, with one scale overlapping the next. When a quill penetrates the skin, every muscle movement of the victim draws it inward, since the angle at which the barbs are set prevents its moving outward.

So many nonsensical ideas still persist about porcupines' shooting quills that we must emphasize the fact that the porcupine does not shoot quills; his quills are loosely attached to his skin, and when they become fastened into the flesh of his enemy they are pulled loose. The porcupine does not fight with pups, but only defends himself.

If a dog were to attack a porcupine directly in front of a veterinarian's office, quill removal would be simple. The doctor would quickly administer an injectable anesthetic and pull the quills. It has never been my good fortune to have a pup quilled within miles of any place where they could be pulled surgically.

Some old hunters, when they have no pliers, just take out their jackknives, cut the quills off, and lead the pup home. They say a cut-off quill is not particularly dangerous and does not work in. Perhaps not so much as whole quills, but I have seen a puppy blinded by a cut-off quill.

No one should take his puppy into a woods where there are known to be porcupines without carrying a pair of pliers that have carefully machined jaws and tips. When a dog has been quilled there is no time to take him to a doctor. Chain him firmly. Get right to work with the pliers from the car if no others are available. With no halfway measure, pull quills, blood or no blood. Here is a situation where heroic methods are necessary.

If quills are allowed to work in out of sight, they will continue to move about the body. Those that entered the front legs or shoulders generally move upward, and by the following morning the needle-sharp points of some can be felt emerging from the skin above the shoulder blades, whence their progress has been guided by the broad bones. Putting dozens or even hundreds of gashes over a pup's shoulders and legs is less satisfactory than letting the quills move themselves to a point where the tips can be felt through the skin. If the point doesn't emerge, nick the skin and pull it, thus removing a fresh crop every day, until they are all out. Feeling for quills is the only efficient method of locating them. X-ray is useless.

Maggots

It is hard to believe that every summer hundreds of pups are killed by flies. And yet puppies are lost everywhere in the United States from being eaten alive by the larvae of flies— maggots. In the North only long-haired dogs are attacked. But in the South, where the screwworm as well as the more common maggot is found, any wound which the animal cannot reach to lick may become infested.

Somewhere under the long bushy coat of a collie, or on the matted hair of a pup, for example, an abrasion occurs. Perhaps it is a small patch of skin disease. Flies are attracted by the serum that the body has exuded and lay eggs on, or in, the wound. Maggots hatch and live on the moist tissue, which they kill by the toxins they secrete. The hair prevents the pup from chewing and licking off these enemies. The maggots continue to grow and spread in the area. Finally some migrate to other moist spots and begin to feed. More flies are attracted, and soon the dog is a mass of maggots.

Even a badly infested pup can be saved by prompt action, but many dogs have died for the want of adequate and timely attention. The coat should be clipped, the holes, which may be an inch deep, washed clean of the pests, and antiseptic dressings applied. Often the first sign to the owner will be prostration of the pup, for the maggots give off a powerful toxin. If you don't discover the worms until that stage has been reached, get the animal to your veterinarian at once. Infusions may save his life.

Screwworms will attack any sore on an animal and eat live tissue. Their damage is like that of the maggots just mentioned. Treatment is the same.

Skunk spraying

Skunk odor has chemically a rather simple formula—a mercaptan, a sort of alcohol-sulphur combination. It is a volatile substance. Volatile chemicals usually turn into gas with heat and maintain their liquid character in cold. The way to dissipate skunk odor, therefore, is to get clothes hot, not to bury them. Hang them in the sun in the summertime, or in a garage attic—anywhere that is dry and hot. The odor leaves quite quickly. A hot bath with lots of soap will usually remove most of the odor from a pup—or from an owner, for that matter. Several baths certainly will. If the dog is left where it is hot, the odor more quickly evaporates to a point where it loses its unpleasantness. After all, it was once used as a basis for fancy perfumes. Washing the pet in tomato juice or canned tomato is quite efficacious in removing the odor. The amount used depends on the size of the puppy.

Drowning

If a pup can be pulled out of the water while his heart is still beating, he can almost always be saved. Slow, steady artificial respiration does the trick. Not as you may have been taught to work on a human, though. Place the animal on his side and push with the flat of the hand on his ribs. Then pull your weight up quickly. Repeat at regular intervals about once in two seconds. He'll usually start to breathe very shallowly, and gradually breathe more deeply. Even when the heartbeat is faint, there is hope. It pays to try.

Electric shock

Since animals' bodies are such excellent conductors of electricity, a shock of 110 volts—which ordinarily merely jolts a human—may kill them. When shocked, they sometimes stiffen so rigidly that they appear to leap into the air. There is a great temptation for a pup to chew a dangling electric cord, and many have been badly injured when they tried it. One such experience is sufficient to teach a pup's owner the hazard of loose electric wires—often at the cost of his pet's life. If the shock has not killed the puppy, artificial respiration should be administered immediately. If he cannot let go of the wire, be careful when you pick him up. He may have urinated; you may step in the urine and, in touching him, the current may pass through you. It is always safer to pull out the plug first or take hold of the wire with a wad of dry cloth and jerk it out of his mouth. Call the veterinarian immediately. When he gets to the animal he will probably administer a drug to stimulate the heart and breathing.

Burns

If you are called upon to treat a burned puppy, clean off all the hair that can mat down on the burned area. Then apply a solution of one part tannic acid to one hundred parts of water (strong, strained tea may be substituted). Then cover gently with vaseline. Your druggist will furnish his best burn remedy and help in an emergency.

Your veterinarian should be called on for all except very minor burns. The anesthetic and treatment he can administer may save your pup. Burns scab over and heal under the scabs if left alone; but sometimes infections grow under the scabs. Tannic acid promotes healthy healing.

If half of a puppy's skin is destroyed by fire, steam, acid, or any agency of burning, it is kindest to put him permanently to sleep. Burned areas usually fail to grow hair, and the period of healing is protracted and painful. Even the duration of shock that usually follows severe burns is long. The owner of any puppy that has been badly burned must always decide quickly, "Is it worth it?"

Fits

The handling of a fit depends upon where it happens and also upon its nature. If a large puppy has a running fit, he may tear through the house, upsetting tables, knickknacks, and chairs, and perhaps end up urinating and defecating on the floor behind the sofa.

You can't stop the fit, but you can reduce the amount of damage the animal may do. He probably won't bite you unless you get in his way. If you can guide him into a room where he can't do serious damage, by all means do so and close the door. Small pups can be laid in a bathtub for the duration of the fit.

Many people, witnessing one of these fits for the first time, feel more terror than the dog. They have visions of being bitten by a mad dog. If you will realize that mad dogs don't have fits from which they recover, but a steady downhill progressive deterioration, it will set your mind at ease if your pet ever has a fit. German shepherds have been known to attack people in the room with them when the fits came on. But most dogs seem fearful of even their masters and will bite only if you try to catch or hold them. Puppies that take fits in the street generally run into yards or under porches, apparently seeking a place to hide.

Let your pup alone until he has recovered from the fit and then look for the cause. Prevention of future attacks is the best first aid. Your veterinarian will help you to locate the cause and provide the cure.

Bruises

It requires a hard, glancing blow to bruise a pup. Even those pups that have been skidded along on a road until the hair was scraped off and the skin left bloody, seldom swell as do some other species. Probably the looseness of the skin over the dog's body is one of its prime protections. When uninfected swellings are found they need only cleansing. They soon subside without further treatment.

If the hair is rubbed off but the skin not cut through, the chances are the healed skin will not be hairless.

Broken bones

You may find, when you examine an injured pup, that he has a broken bone. A broken leg is the most common animal fracture and requires immediate attention. Its care involves straightening the leg and immobilizing it. Sometimes this takes courage. A splint is needed. A tine from a bamboo rake, a yardstick, may serve as an improvised splint. The leg should be tied to the splint below and above the break and wrapped with anything suitable to hold it securely in place until you can get the pup to the veterinarian.

A splint should be applied at once. If the broken bone slashes about the flesh, it can easily cut a major vein or artery, and then the area around the break will become a large pocket filled with blood, greatly complicating the task of setting. It is just as important to splint a greenstick fracture, because movement or a fall may break it further.

If ribs are broken, keep the puppy quiet. It is possible for ribs to puncture lungs, so lay him down with the broken ribs up and keep him as calm as possible until the veterinarian arrives.

A fractured pelvis heals slowly. Little can be done to repair pelvic breaks or to hasten the natural process of reconstruction. Occasionally only one side is broken and the pup can continue to walk on three legs. More often the pelvis is fractured in such a way as to preclude walking until the usual numbness develops and anesthetizes the area. For several days after the break the puppy may be unable to raise himself without help. Gradually he takes a few unstable steps and soon is waddling about. Don't expect him to run for at least a month after the break. Even after the healing is well started it may be necessary to help him up, carry him outside, and sometimes hold him in a position to defecate. Some pups learn why they are taken outside surprisingly soon and, as quickly as they are placed in position, will void. Standing the pup up and putting pressure on the bladder from both sides usually causes urination, and it is not uncommon to have a pup so cooperative that just touching his sides is suggestion enough for him to urinate.

One of the most usual back breaks comes at the point inside the body where the tail vertebrae start. In such a fracture the tail hangs limp and lifeless. It is often soiled with feces because the puppy cannot raise it to defecate. Sometimes there is enough muscular strength left to move it slightly. If it is not set, it may retain its life. More often the tail loses all its feeling and dries up with dry gangrene. In this case your veterinarian will have to open the skin over the break and remove the useless appendage.

Bee stings

It s not uncommon to hear of pups being stung to death by bees. They will frequently swell from single stings and more often come home drooling with mouths partly open from pain and swelling occasioned by snapping up a stinging insect—wasp, hornet, or bee.

The painful stings, the poisonous effect of the toxin, and worst of all, the sensitivity of the foreign material developed by having been previously stung may produce a shock. But the swelling subsides, and the shock is soon over. There is usually nothing to be too alarmed about in bee stings.

Poisoning

Pain, trembling, panting, vomiting, convulsions, coma, slimy mouths are all symptoms of poisoning. Any of these, except a caustically burned mouth, may also be a symptom of another malady. But if your pup should manifest any of these symptoms, you should investigate immediately to see if he has been poisoned.

Animals are very seldom deliberately poisoned. Usually they are poisoned either by chewing on plants that have been sprayed, by gnawing at a piece of wood which has some paint pigment on it, by catching a ground mole which has been poisoned with cyanide, by consuming poison put out for other animals or insects, or by eating infected garbage. Since none of the poisons is easily traced, you ought to know the procedure to follow in case your pet becomes poisoned.

An emetic must be administered immediately. The loss of a few minutes may give the poison time to do irremediable damage. Mix equal parts of hydrogen peroxide and water. Force your pup to take one tablespoonful, if he is a ten-pound puppy, and more if he is larger. A forty-pound puppy needs about two ounces. In two or three minutes the contents of his stomach will have been regurgitated.

Either mustard or a strong salt solution can be used as an emetic, but hydrogen peroxide has proved to be most effective.

Following the administration of this emetic, call your veterinarian. If you know the source of the poisoning and can look at the package it came from, you will find the antidote on the label. If you don't know the poison to which your pet has been exposed, your veterinarian will probably identify it from its symptoms and give further appropriate treatment.

If there is any chance that poison can be the cause of intestinal trouble, it is imperative that all traces of the poison be eliminated before giving the animal drugs that will stop bowel movement and allow the intestines to become quiescent— paregoric, for instance. But if the intestines are badly corroded, it is dangerous to give violent physics.

HOUSEHOLD ANTIDOTES FOR COMMON POISONS

POISON	ANTIDOTE
Acids: Hydrochloric; nitric; acetic	Bicarbonate of soda; eggshells; crushed plaster (tablespoonful)
Alkalies: Sink cleansers; cleaning agent	Vinegar or lemon juice (several tablespoonfuls)
Arsenic: Lead arsenate; calcium arsenate; white arsenic; paris green	Epsom salts (1 teaspoonful in water)
Hydrocyanic Acid: Wild cherry; laurel leaves	Glucose (2 tablespoonfuls dextrose or corn syrup)
Lead: Lead arsenic; paint pigments	Epsom salts (1 teaspoonful in water)
Phosphorus: Rat poison	Peroxide of hydrogen. (Peroxide and water in equal parts, 1 oz. to each 10 pounds of weight of animal)
Mercury: Bichloride of mercury	Eggs and milk
Theobromine: Cooking chocolate	Pentobarbital, phenobarbital
Thallium: Bug poisons	Table salt (1 teaspoonful in water)
Food Poisoning: Bacteria from garbage or decomposed food	Peroxide of hydrogen. Give enema after stomach has emptied
Strychnine: Strychnine sulfate in rodent and animal poisons	Sedatives such as phenobarbital, Nembutal (1 grain to 7 pounds of dog)
Sedatives: Overdoses in medicating	Strong coffee (1 cupful for a 40-pound dog)
DDT: Flea powders; bug poisons	Peroxide of hydrogen and enema. No antidote known

Once the offending material is removed, your job is to give such common home remedies as milk of bismuth, paregoric, strong tea for its tannic-acid content. Strangely enough, some cases are benefited by castor oil, which removes the cause and tends to be followed by constipation. Veterinarians can prescribe sulfaguanidine and sulfathalidine and other prescription drugs.

The same drugs which are useful in human care can be employed for puppies. Today a variety of mixtures embodying kaolin, bismuth, and pectin are available, and your veterinarian will advise you on their use.

General advice in treating poisoning

Immediate action is essential. Some poisons are absorbed at once. Empty the stomach first, give the antidote second, then hurry your puppy to the veterinarian.

GIVING MEDICINES, APPLYING ACCESSORIES

All dog owners should know how to administer the common drugs used with puppies, how to give their pets medicine in liquid and capsule form, how to apply the standard bandages, how to take the temperatures of animals—in short, how to handle all the little problems of caring for a sick or injured pet.

Your veterinarian will diagnose your pup's condition, prescribe the proper medication, and tell you the kind of care and attention your pet needs. That alone is not enough to restore the animal to health. In most cases you will treat your pet at home, and it is your responsibility to carry out the veterinarian's instructions. The most effective drug ever prescribed will not help your puppy if you cannot manage to get more than 5 percent of the dose down his throat. If you allow the pup to remove the bandage the veterinarian has applied, and permit him to expose an open wound to infection simply because you don't know how to apply a bandage that will stay, you can hardly expect a quick and satisfactory recovery.

Your veterinarian will outline a course of treatment for your sick pet, but the way you carry out his instructions and the care you give the animal will usually determine how effective the treatment will be. If you can give the doctor the kind of intelligent cooperation that he has a right to expect, your pup's chances for recovery will be greatly increased.

Liquids

Whenever a liquid is to be given, you should always remember that if certain liquids enter the lungs they can be very dangerous. The first question you should ask yourself is: What would happen if the animal inhaled some?

Pure water solutions of quickly soluble drugs are least dangerous. Hydrogen peroxide turns to water and oxygen when it decomposes in the fizzing effect known to everyone. On the other hand, milk, which is sometimes used as a base or vehicle for drugs, contains solids. Fat is one of them, and fat in the lungs is especially dangerous. If the drug used is harmless if it gets into the lungs—that is, if it is a water solution—it is fairly safe to fill the puppy's mouth and throat and force him to swallow it. If some of the medicine trickles down the windpipe, the only unfortunate thing that can happen is a blast of the medicine in your face or on your coat sleeve when the patient coughs. But when a solution dangerous to the lungs is to be administered, a little at a time had best be given.

In either event there are two practical ways of giving a liquid medicine: the lip-pocket method and by stomach tube. Let's see how and when each of these is used.

The Lip-Pocket Method. Although an experienced person

can accomplish this alone, you will probably find that two people are necessary for satisfactory results. Place the pup on a table broadside to you. Make him sit. Tilt his head back so that he is looking at the ceiling. With your right hand hold his chin in this position. Slide the fingers of your left hand under his lip, push back and catch hold of the angle where lower and upper lips join. Pull this out and upward. Now you have a cup or pocket which will hold a considerable amount. While you hold the patient thus, your assistant pours the medicine or liquid food into the pocket, giving a ten-pound pup perhaps a teaspoonful. As it runs between his teeth and onto the back of the tongue, he will swallow it. When this is gone, more is poured in, and soon he has the whole dose. A word of caution: the assistant should stand out of the line of fire, for if the puppy coughs, he or she is liable to be thoroughly sprayed.

If an especially resistant pup is being dosed, the assistant has another duty. With one hand he holds both front paws firmly so that the pup can't pull them loose, and with the other he pours the medicine into the lip pocket.

The Stomach-Tube Method. What seems a great task is in reality a simple and safe method if two people cooperate to dose a puppy. A piece of rubber tubing, one eighth inch inside diameter and twelve inches long, is large enough for a puppy. You can get both the tube and a syringe—either glass or rubber will do—at your druggist's. The syringe should be filled with the medicine and left within reach. When you are ready to insert the tube, hold the animal as described above with the head straight up. As the tube is pushed over the back of the tongue into the throat, the patient will gulp and swallow it down. If it has been moistened, it will slide down the gullet with reasonable ease.

There is one danger to guard against. You must be extremely careful not to get the tube into the windpipe, for if fluids are squirted down the tube into the lungs by mistake, the results may be tragic. By holding the upper end of the tube close to your ear, you can tell whether the other end is in the windpipe by the purring sound of air rushing in and out of the tube. If the tube has entered the gullet properly, you will not hear any sound at all. Feeling the throat is another method of being sure where the tube is. The windpipe is in front and closest to the skin, and in puppies which are not too fat you should have no difficulty in feeling the tube in the gullet behind it.

When you are certain that the tube is where it should be, have your assistant, who needs both hands for the job, connect the syringe to the tube and squirt the medicine or liquid food down the tube. In mature animals the stomach tube may be left in for several minutes without causing strangulation; the patient goes right on breathing normally.

This stomach-tube method is particularly useful in feeding tiny puppies which are too cold or too weak to suck. I have saved dozens this way and have taught many assistants to do it, using a urinary catheter, or small rubber tube. It is a quick way of feeding, and one that is most useful in supplementing an inadequate maternal milk supply. To be sure, you must always be certain that the tube is in the gullet, but that is not hard to determine once you have done it a few times. When you consider that at the clinic we have reared whole litters of puppies experimentally in this fashion, it is easy to see that one man who passes a tube on a litter of eight, five times a day, or a total of 280 times a week, must not experience too much difficulty.

You should never try to squirt a drug into your pup's mouth, snap it shut, and expect the animal to swallow it. Most of the solution runs out. The animal shakes his head and the administration is a failure. You can sometimes overcome the patient's dislike for some drugs by disguising them in sweet syrups thinned down. Glucose (dextrose) is often administered to advantage to sick animals but, if given in the form of corn syrup, it is difficult to pour. It must be thinned. If any sweet substance is given carefully and without a struggle, the subsequent dosages will be simpler, and pups in particular can often be trained to open their mouths and take it without a fuss. I have seen many that soon were willing to lick the syrup from a tablespoon.

Pills and capsules

It doesn't require sleight of hand to get a pill or capsule down the throat of a pup, even when the pet resists. It's all in knowing how. Opening the animal's mouth, dropping in the medicine, closing his mouth, and rubbing his throat may work now and then, but it's not a sure enough method to rely on.

With the left hand (if you're right-handed) grasp the top of the puppy's muzzle and pull his head upward. Squeeze the thumb on one side and the fingers on the other, thereby pushing the lips over the teeth and partly opening the mouth. Your patient won't close his mouth, because to do so he will have to bite his lips. With your right hand pick up the pill or capsule between the thumb and first or second finger and with the little finger pull down the lower jaw. Hold it open with the side of the little finger and drop the pill as far back on the tongue as possible. With your forefinger, or with the forefinger and second finger, push the pill gently but quickly as far back into the throat as you can. Then withdraw your hand quickly, let the mouth close and hold it together until the pup sticks out his tongue in the act of swallowing. Several pills and capsules may be poked down in this way at one time.

Some capsules contain bitter or choking drugs. If a pup bites them, they may cause him fright, suffocation, and a taste so obnoxious that he will try for many minutes to cough or scratch it out. If you are giving your pet medicine of this sort, you will want to be certain that no capsules are dropped between his teeth or insufficiently pushed down his throat.

Puppies of short-nosed breeds, such as Boston terriers, boxers, English bulldogs, bull mastiffs, have such fat tongues and restricted throats that laymen frequently have difficulty in properly medicating them. The pills or capsules become slippery when wet and slide around sideways over the back of the broad tongue. It is wise never to try to give wet pills, especially wet capsules. If you are unsuccessful in the first attempt to give the medicine, take the capsule out and dry it. It will often stick to your finger just enough to enable you to pilot it into the back of the throat properly. Sometimes two fingers can keep it from sliding sideways.

Bandages and their use

Of the many kinds of bandage used by physicians and nurses, only a few are very useful in veterinary work. Rolls of muslin and gauze, many-tailed bandages, and adhesive are those needed. Anyone can rip an old sheet into three-inch-wide strips to make a bandage in a pinch. But those strips had best be rolled tightly before applying. Two three- or four-inch bandages, six feet long, will usually be sufficient to bandage any pup.

Many-tails are simply strips of cloth as wide as the area to be bandaged on the patient and torn in the same number of parallel strips from each end toward the central area.

Adhesive tape one inch wide should serve almost any purpose. To cover a wide area it may be lapped, and if a narrower strip is desired, it may easily be ripped.

Most bandages will be applied by the home veterinarian for minor cuts and blemishes, or as stopgap measures before taking the pup to the veterinarian, after which, if bandaging is necessary, the veterinarian will instruct the client as to how he wants the bandage applied in the future. This may save the client further trips to the veterinarian.

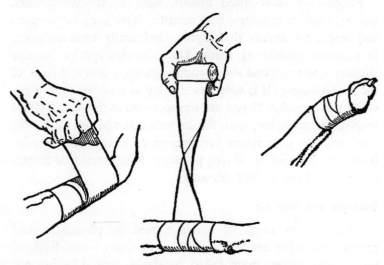

How to apply a bandage. A smooth job can be done if you reverse the roll occasionally. Right, pressure bandage to stop blood flow. Usually these bandages are applied too loosely.

The most common use of bandages in puppies is to prevent self-injury. Suppose a pup has been caught in a steel trap. He is found before the part of the leg below the trap bit has died. The skin has been cleaned, and the veterinarian has sutured it. If he is not prevented from licking it, he will remove the stitches and open the wound. Moreover, after the bandage is applied, there will be considerable weeping from the wound, and despite antiseptics, an odd odor will develop. This is not a bad sign but rather a good one. The pup smells it and becomes frantic to lick it, since there is something about the odor which animals either enjoy or which excites them to lick. At any rate, they may rip bandages off, necessitating application of new ones fairly often.

In covering such an area, several things must be kept in mind. The bandage cannot be wound too tightly or circulation will be impeded, and the area below it will swell from blood and lymph. It must be wound tightly enough not to slip. If swelling occurs, the bandage may be cut but not necessarily removed. New adhesive must then be wound around it.

First some surgical dressing—powder, solution, or salve— is applied, and usually a sponge of several thicknesses of gauze put over it. The bandage is unrolled about the wound firmly until several thicknesses have been applied. The end is torn lengthwise to make two tails, which are tied in a knot at the bottom of the tear and then wound around the leg in opposite directions and tied in a knot again. When the bandage fails to go on smoothly, or when it is necessary to go from a thin place on the leg to a thicker section, if the roll is twisted occasionally, as shown in the illustration, it will go on with professional smoothness. If one layer of adhesive tape is then applied, making sure that at least one half inch sticks to the hair above the bandage, it will hold the bandage material in place and be sufficient protection against the patient's efforts to remove it.

One of the most frequent uses made of bandages is to check blood flow. In this case we call them pressure bandages. Puppies often cut their feet on glass, tin cans, or other sharp objects. Since the feet are extremely vascular (full of blood vessels), even a small cut may bleed enough to leave a large blood spot everywhere the pup steps. Cuts higher on the foot can cause sufficient hemorrhage to make a pup anemic, but I have never seen one bleed to death from such a gash.

To stop the flow of blood, apply a small cloth sponge directly to the cut and quickly wind a bandage tightly about the foot many times. It may become red from blood soaking through it, but it will slowly stop bleeding.

Tourniquets are so often recommended to stop bleeding in human beings that puppy owners sometimes resort to them injudiciously. With a pup, a strong elastic band can suffice, or even thumb pressure over the cut artery. If a tourniquet of any sort is applied to a whole limb, it is important that it be released occasionally to let blood in and out of the part tied off.

Many-tailed bandages are usually used about the body. When pups scratch and chew holes in themselves because of skin infections, there is often no better accessory treatment. Skin remedies are applied and the bandage put on. Depending upon how much of the body it is to cover, the bandage generally has two or four holes cut to allow the legs to go through. Then a row of knots is tied along the back and left in bows, so that it can be untied to remove the bandage, which may be used again. Long surgical incisions on the sides, back, or belly can sometimes be kept covered by many-tails. Head operations, ear troubles, such as splits or sutured ear flaps, can best be protected with many-tails.

Using thermometers

Ordinary rectal thermometers, which one can purchase in any drugstore, are adequate for taking the temperatures of pups. It is a simple matter to shake one down, then dip it in vaseline or mineral oil, and insert it three quarters of its length into the rectum. It should be left in for more than sixty seconds, removed, wiped clean with a piece of cotton, and read. Don't wash it in hot water; anyone can read such a thermometer by twisting it slowly until the wide silver stripe appears and reading the figures opposite the top of the column. Most thermometers are graduated in fifths, and since each fifth

equals two tenths, the reading is usually expressed in tenths—
i.e., 102⅕ degrees F. is 102.2 degrees F. A puppy's normal
temperature is from 101 to 102 degrees.

PART FIVE

SURGERY

Puppies of some breeds must have their tails shortened,
some usually have their extra toes removed, and some, custom
and styling decreeing, must have their ears cropped. A great
many puppies of all breeds are neutered (not neutralized), un-
sexed, whichever term you prefer, or, applied to females,
spayed (not spaded), and to males, castrated (not casterized,
cauterized, casterated). Many puppies have congenital hernias
which must be repaired. All these surgical procedures are done
in the normal course of things. Being an old dog breeder, I
believe that only the neutering operation and hernia repairs
are necessary. True, the artistic surgery gives a zip to the
dog's appearance, but there's a lot in what we are used to. We
formerly were used to Boston and bull terriers with trimmed
ears; now they look fine with erect natural ears, and so would
all the other cropped-ear breeds. And if only breeders would
select for small erect ears, the boxers, Doberman pinschers,
and Great Danes soon would not need ear cropping.

Tail trimming

Most veterinarians know what lengths the tails of all of the
tail-docked breeds should be. If your veterinarian does not,
because his practice is chiefly with farm stock, then you can
show him this chart, and he can dock the tail to the generally
accepted length.

Tail trimming is usually done on about the fifth or sixth day of the puppy's life. At that time, too, extra toes are snipped off.

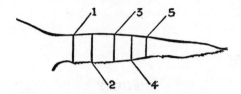

Points at which puppies' tails are usually docked. The lengths shown are those generally preferred, but styles change. If any doubt exists as to the proper length for your breed, consult the breed standard. (1) American fox terriers, boxers, Doberman pinschers. (2) Welsh corgi. (3) All spaniels. (4) German short-haired pointer, Lakeland terrier. (5) Airedale, wire-haired fox terrier, English smooth fox terrier, poodle.

If your puppy wasn't given the benefits of such artistry before you got him, then you need to know what follows; if he was, skip it.

Dewclaws

There is seldom any need to have the front dewclaws removed. Some poodle breeders have them taken off so as to exhibit clean front legs on their show dogs. Nearly all the other breeds are never touched. Dewclaws are a hereditary appendage. If the rear legs have them, and they look unsightly, dangling loosely, it is just as well to have them removed. Left on hunting hounds, dewclaws constitute a real trouble spot, especially in the North where they often are cut by crust. The nails in dewclaws grow as fast as the other nails, but because they do not touch the ground, the nails do not wear off and usually grow in a circle, penetrating the toe and causing annoyance and pain. Unless you can keep these nails trimmed, it costs less and hurts less in the long run to have your veterinarian surgically remove such toes.

Hernias

Many a puppy owner is alarmed at finding a small or large, soft roundish lump protruding from his puppy's navel. It is an umbilical hernia. Whether or not it needs surgical attention depends on the size of the opening in the abdominal muscles that failed to heal across. If your puppy has such a lump, squeeze it until the contents are forced back into the abdomen. Then feel the size of the hole. If it is over three sixteenths of an inch across, there is a possibility that a loop of intestine could work out through that opening and become strangulated. If that happens, a very serious operation is required. Such hernias should be repaired. If the hole is small, and only the omentum—the broad, veil-like tissue in the abdomen—fills the hernia, this will generally become hardened into a firm lump which may as well be forgotten unless it appears unsightly.

Tumors

Tumors in young puppies are not reported, but in some breeds, boxers especially, at about five or six months of age there is a highly malignant tumor that appears on the skin as an oval red lump. It should be removed as early as possible. I have seen a large number, and experience shows that if they are not removed while small, they soon appear in many places.

Another form of tumor which gives puppy owners great concern is the mouth papilloma, a small whitish growth, looking like a tiny straw flower, which appears in the mouth either singly or in great numbers. It may be found at times around the eyes, too, and I have found them in other places on puppies' bodies.

Papillomas are caused by a virus. They are only temporary growths and, if left alone, will drop off. But when there are many in the mouth, food catches in them and causes foul breath and annoyance to the puppy. I removed 256 from one puppy. Nearly two months are required for the disease to run its course, and the tumors drop off if left undisturbed.

Ear cropping

It is fast becoming "the thing to do" to let the puppy buyer have the ears cropped, with all the trouble which that process entails. If you have a boxer, Dane, or Doberman which needs cropping, and you want to be as humane as possible, then have the pup cropped before it is nine weeks old. True, it can be done any time, but the older the puppy is, the harder it is on the pup and the more trouble for you and the veterinarian. There are a number of methods, one of which (the emascula-tome method, which I originated) is practically bloodless. Sparing blood in young puppies is important to their health, so if you have any choice in ear croppers, choose the man who can do the job as bloodlessly as possible.

Neutering

This looms large in the consideration not only of the sex of puppy to buy but whether to have the operation done when the time comes. Here are the arguments for and against:

Considerable research now shows that spaying has little effect on the general characteristics of the animal. Spayed greyhounds race as well as unspayed and have very little tendency to be fatter than unspayed sisters. If the operation is done properly, other species are not spoiled, except for reproduction purposes.

This is true with one qualification—that the operation be done when the animal is nearly full grown or later. This is very important. Studies show that when animals are spayed very young there is a disharmony in their glandular development. If it is desirable to produce a chicken that will be large, awkward, lazy, and fat—a capon—the operation is not put off until the bird is full grown. If it were, the result would be merely a sterile rooster. No, the operation is done in the early life of the bird, because at that time it accomplishes precisely the changes that we want to avoid in spayed pets. Exactly the same thing is true of bitches. A spayed puppy becomes neither male nor female in appearance and grows very fat. The waddling, turtlelike, lazy, spayed bitches are usually those that were spayed as puppies.

The fact that some spayed bitches get fat is not in itself a valid argument against spaying. Unspayed bitches, too, get fat. Some of the most grossly overweight dogs I know are whole animals. They are overfed. If they had been spayed and placed in the hands of the same owner, his or her explanation for the overweight condition would have been that the bitch had been spayed.

It is now believed that spaying has little effect upon a mature animal. The animal does not have mating cycles and the urges which they bring. This may have a very slight effect on weight and personality. Spaying in babyhood causes abnormal development. The only reason for spaying bitches young is to prevent the bitches of vicious breeds from becoming dangerous as they get older. If they are spayed as puppies, they tend to remain gentle.

Spaying a bitch has a number of definite advantages:

1. The animal is spared the risk attending birth.

2. The owner is spared raising or having to destroy unwanted animals.

3. The owner avoids the annoyance of males surrounding his home, killing shrubbery, breaking windows, and following members of his family.

4. The spayed female does not wander at certain seasons as the unspayed does.

5. Spaying almost certainly prevents the formation of can-

cer in the breast, which sometimes occurs in bitches three or four years of age and commonly in older dogs. It also prevents metritis, an affliction of unspayed bitches.

6. The owner is saved perhaps forty dollars a year for boarding his pet twice a year.

7. Food is saved, since a pregnant, or lactating, mother consumes more food than a spayed one.

8. In many places the license fee for a spayed bitch is less than for an unspayed bitch. Where this is so, the owner will save the cost of spaying many times.

There are also disadvantages in spaying:

1. An owner may someday regret that his female can't reproduce.

2. As spayed animals grow older they sometimes lose control of the bladder sphincter. But this can be corrected by giving a drug—stilbestrol—occasionally.

Does spaying harm a hunting dog? Some of the greatest hunters ever known have been spayed bitches. In fact, it helps hunting dogs, because unspayed bitches so often come in heat in the all-too-short hunting season. Because of this they often miss the training and experience that makes better hunters of the spayed bitches which are never incapacitated.

Much the same arguments hold for castration as for spaying. Generally it is done to make males stay home. Those which congregate around the abode of a bitch come home punctured with tooth marks from the frequent fracases attending such meetings. Such dogs frequently wander away and are brought home by the dog warden, who collects his fee. They are expensive animals. Castration usually alters their wandering habits, because the sex urge is often the cause of it.

There are many other reasons for castrating animals. Dogs of breeds whose members tend to become vicious with age are often rendered gentle and lovable when castrated young. Castration also tends to prevent indiscriminate wetting and thus saves shrubbery.

It seems to be the opinion of many that animals should not be spayed or castrated because copulation is essential to health. This is not the case. Any animal, whether whole, spayed, or castrated, is just as healthy if it is never bred as those which are used for breeding. Considering the risks of pregnancy and birth, a spayed female's chances for longer life are actually greater. As for males, only a small percentage ever copulate in their whole lives. This is true of many species, not of our pet animals alone.

PART SIX

EXERCISING AND GROOMING YOUR PUPPY

The plain truth is that no puppy needs any more exercise than he gets in a pen six by ten feet in dimension. It is nice to give him more—his leg muscles will be better developed— but it is not essential to exercise him. The best part of it is that taking him for a walk exercises you.

Many people, when they say *exercise* a dog, mean taking him for a walk where he can evacuate and urinate. If you had seen as many thousands of happy puppies of all sizes—even Saint Bernards—grow to full size in runs eight by twenty feet, you would realize how little exercise puppies *need*. I have raised hundreds of beagles and cocker spaniels in wire-bottom runs three by six feet, and because they never knew anything else, they have been supremely happy.

But I said *need*, not how much puppies can stand. I have taken five-month-old puppies, which were raised in eight-by-twenty-foot pens, for six-mile walks the first time they ever left their pens and have been amazed at their endurance. But then few persons realize how much a mature dog can stand. Sled dogs, six to a team, pull sleds with ton loads miles and miles a day. Foxhounds have been known to run forty-eight hours pursuing foxes and during that time may run well over three hundred miles.

So exercise, while not necessary, is most pleasant. And there are simple, useful ways to exercise your puppy. If he is a hunter, get him into the woods and fields to accustom him to the environment that he will come to love. If he is a retriever, teach him to fetch. Go to an open place and throw a ball. Fifty yards is a short retrieve. While you stand in one place, the pup runs one hundred yards for each throw. Seventeen retrieves, and he has run a mile.

If you live near a golf links, teach your pup to retrieve a golf ball. When he has learned that, take him around the rough of the course, make believe you are throwing the ball, and he will dash away soon returning with a golf ball in his mouth. I have a friend whose cocker spaniel brought him forty-two balls in a few hours.

Puppies of larger breeds can be taught to pull wagons or sleds by the time they are six months old. Some puppies love to swim and will bring out sticks the owner throws into the water.

If you have no natural way to exercise your pup, don't worry; he'll be just about as healthy with none.

Probably rough playing gives puppies all the exercise they need. Some puppies will play with you, some with toys which they will toss into the air, wrestle with, then chew on. Give your pup plently of playtime and encourage playing up to the point where he bites too sharply. Old rag dolls make excellent playthings. Even a well-knotted towel amuses some pups for hours. If you give him a rubber toy, be sure he doesn't chew it apart and swallow the pieces. During teething, pups love to chew, and chewing becomes almost play with them. Encourage it throughout teething—from three and a half to six months of age—but stop it if the puppy uses his second teeth where he shouldn't.

COMBING AND BRUSHING

It is well to realize that by properly combing and brushing your pup you can do a lot toward his training. This is especially important in the case of breeds like cockers, poodles, all the wirehairs, setters, and long-haired breeds in general. When these puppies are small and easily controlled, you can teach them that grooming tools won't hurt them; even get them to enjoy being groomed. Watch a dog at a dog show being groomed. He will stand like a statue while the handler goes over him.

Set your puppy on a table at arm's length. Never hug him while you work on him. After a while you can stand back and view him from all sides, while the pup stands because he enjoys it. Use a strong comb with teeth of the proper spacing for a dog of your pup's breed. Professionals generally use one with twelve teeth to the inch, and teeth one inch long. Push the teeth right down to the skin and comb until no knots remain. You can pull them out quite easily from puppy coats or, if they are too tenuous, cut them lengthwise with scissors and then comb. If you have a long-haired pup which brings in twigs, leaves, and in general gets easily snarled, you must comb often. But by all means be the boss, and if the puppy objects, don't stop combing. Many a pup has learned that he can bluff his owner by objecting to combing and in this way is easily trained to become a vicious dog. If, however, he does object, place a tie about his face and finish the job once you start it.

Sometimes a puppy may need to be held in place by a cord from above attached to his collar. It is usually possible to arrange such a cord, which can be shortened as he grows. This can be done by putting a table in a doorway. Affix a hook to the top of the doorway and drop a cord from it to the puppy's collar.

CLIPPING

If your pup is a cocker, poodle, wire, Airedale, or other dog which needs trimming or plucking, accustom him to stand on a table like a show dog, where he will be independent. The person who clips for you will appreciate this early training.

Poodles are ordinarily clipped on the face and feet by the time they are four or five months old and some even younger, at six and eight weeks. Some breeds for showing are always plucked on the body and clipped on the heads. Here is no place to debate the advantages of plucking or clipping of the dog kept only as a pet. Plucking advocates will object, but after seeing the satisfaction expressed by literally thousands of owners of wire-haired breeds after their dogs were clipped, and for less than half what it would have cost to pluck them, I am unqualifiedly in favor of clipping. For show dogs, I'm opposed to it.

NAIL CARE

If only to save nylons or prevent runs in sweaters and so forth, a puppy's nails should be kept trimmed. But there are other reasons, most important of which is the effect long nails have on a pup's feet. If the nails are allowed to grow too long, the toes will become tipped upward, which in turn will cause some pain and also a foot that does not develop naturally.

In a long-haired dog long nails will frequently catch in his ears when he scratches himself. Sometimes the pads of the foot actually overgrow, so that instead of a good hard surface the front of the pad will appear spongy, and this overgrowth will need to be trimmed off frequently—a practice that is never necessary if the nails are kept short.

Your veterinarian will trim them for you, or you can buy a pair of clippers and keep them trimmed at home. In young pups it is a simple matter to trim off the hook or transparent part. But as the puppy grows it is not so easy to know where the "quick" begins and where the nail will bleed. At this point there are nerves, so the puppy will let you know when you are too close.

If you have patience and time, use a nail file and keep the nails filed off. A good rule is to have the nail just long enough to touch the ground when the dog is standing. Many dog owners keep their pets' nails filed. Dogs running on concrete keep their own nails filed. Only their dewclaw nails grow too long because those nails do not reach the ground to wear off.

What if you trim the nails too closely and they bleed? No harm whatever comes of it except the damage the blood does to the floors or to your clothing. In fact, the toenails of some breeds of dog, if they are allowed to grow too long, will nearly always bleed when they are cut off to the correct length. This applies particularly to bull terriers and several other terrier breeds, where the blood seems to come almost to the tip of the nail no matter how long it grows. The nails of such dogs should be kept filed at regular intervals.

If a veterinarian cuts your dog's nails, and they bleed, you will notice that he wraps the foot in a bandage and tells you to wait until you get home to remove it. Be sure to keep the dog off concrete for a day, because this will wear the end off the nail and cause it to start bleeding again.

If you cut the nails yourself, and they bleed, be sure to cover them for a while with bandage until bleeding stops. When the bandage is removed keep him from walking or running on cement or stones for a few hours.

CARE OF THE EARS

Young puppies seldom need to have their ears cleaned.

Dirty ear canals may be brought to your attention in several ways. One way you may become aware of this condition is to have your pup shake his head and scratch at his ears a great deal of the time, or you may notice a heavy, dark, waxy discharge. Another indication is a strong odor that exudes from certain infections.

Many products are presently being used very successfully for ear-cleaning purposes. Propylene glycol is one such material.

Place the pup on a table or raised place. Take an ear flap in your left hand so that the ear canal is exposed and pour enough propylene glycol in the ear canal to almost completely fill it with fluid. Massage the base of the ear and take up the fluid which runs out of the ear with a small piece of cotton.

Propylene glycol can be obtained at any drugstore, or your veterinarian may prescribe some other medication which is equally effective for dissolving wax in the ear canal.

Poodles, Kerry blues, and many of the wire-haired breeds grow hair in the ear canals. This hair must be kept pulled out or it becomes matted with wax, and canker develops. Strangely enough, there is no pain associated with its removal. The puppy seems to enjoy it. All you need is a pair of forceps. Pointed electrical pincers will do if none of surgical type are available. A great deal can be extracted with the thumb and finger because the hair loosens quite easily.

ANAL GLANDS

Every puppy has a pair of glands, which are part of his skin, located on either side of and just below the opening of his anus. These are called the anal glands. When the puppy becomes terrified, each gland discharges its contents through a tiny tube or duct. If the pup never has a good fright, the glands may become infected, and the puppy will sit down and drag himself along by his front legs—playing sleigh ride, as the children call it. If this performance fails to squeeze the contents out, an infection may produce an abscess that ruptures through the skin after first swelling greatly and causing pain.

Your veterinarian will show you how to empty the glands. If he is not near you, try it this way: Feel with your thumb and second finger to determine the location of the pair of swollen glands. They may feel like a pair of small marbles. Cover your hand with a piece of cotton. Hold the pup's tail straight up with your left hand, squeeze with your right thumb and finger, through the cotton, until you have forced all the glands' contents out through the anus on to the cotton. This material will have a most obnoxious odor. If you get any on your hand, wash it off quickly, or your hand will smell for a long while.

TEETHING AND TOOTH CARE

Look into the puppy's mouth often and watch the development of his teeth. The sharp little puppy teeth begin to shed when the pup is about fourteen weeks of age. The two upper-middle incisors fall out first. It takes about two months before the new teeth are all in. You may find some of the puppy teeth around the house; he probably has swallowed the rest. No harm done.

Should your puppy have any disease during the teething period, you can expect his teeth to be pitted, due to a lack of enamel being deposited while the teeth were growing. An experienced veterinarian can look at a dog's teeth and be able to tell you which weeks of the pup's life he was sick. The structure of the tooth grows, but no enamel is deposited until the disease is over. And if one knows the time when the various teeth grow in, one will see how these telltale marks furnish a timetable. The discolored pits or bands remain for the puppy's life.

Fortunately, puppies' teeth seldom need cleaning; that task is reserved for later in their lives.

A quite common teething trouble is the failure of the canine teeth—the fangs—to fall out when the new ones come in. This may cause irritations on the lips if the first teeth are pushed out sideways, but usually the only harm done is that food catches between the old and new teeth. Have your veterinarian remove the teeth that fail to drop out.

BATHING

It seems incredible that nearly every dog owner believes it is wrong to bathe a puppy, or let it get wet, until the pup is six months old. No one likes to advise on such a point because of the usual unscientific method of thinking that causes too many people to feel that because one event follows another, the first is the cause of the second. If I advise a client to bathe her dog, and a week later the pup has pneumonia, I am to blame—I and the bath. Therefore I do not advise you. I can say I've never known of a bath in a warm home, after which the pup was dried, to cause pneumonia, and I have known of hundreds of cases of pneumonia in puppies which had not had baths, or been exposed. On the basis of my experience, it is much more likely that a puppy will develop pneumonia if he is not given a bath.

But, to be sensible, we all know a dog was born soaking wet and dried from his own body heat and that of his mother. If one of my puppies gets dirty or smelly, I bathe him, but not before.

Today there are many ways of bathing puppies. You can use special dog soap, cake or liquid. Or you can use baby soaps, or household soaps, cake or liquid. You can give him a "dry bath" by using a special preparation made in any of several ways. These are usually detergents in which bug-killing drugs are incorporated. Some leave an insecticidal residue, some do not. Some are of a dry, corn-meal-powder base, some of foaming whipped-cream consistency.

Bathing is accomplished by selecting a proper place to start with. The size and condition of the dog help to determine the place. A month-old Chihuahua may be washed in a teacup, while a six-month-old Saint Bernard needs nothing smaller than the family bathtub. If you don't mind using the tub after the dog, you can use your own. Thousands of dog owners do. Or you can rig up a special tub for your pet. Some owners wash their dogs standing on the lawn, using a pail of water.

The first thing to do if you are giving a water bath is to get the soap ready. Suppose you decide on flakes. Put a handful of flakes in a pan of warm water and dissolve them. Have another pan with warm water in which is mixed some insect-killing drug, of which several are available. Put a cotton plug in each ear of your pet, and he will be less inclined to shake himself. Also put on an apron of some waterproof material to protect yourself in the event the dog struggles or shakes.

The experienced owner realizes that water runs off his dog's back and only slowly wets the hair and penetrates to the skin. Soap is a wetting agent. Therefore he soaps the dog as he wets him. I like to use 20 percent liquid soap and pour a line of it along the animal's back. I apply water to the soap, and the mixture at once wets the whole coat. I then work up a lather by rubbing and rinse the dog thoroughly, making sure all the soap is washed out of the coat. If there is still dirt to be seen or the odor is not gone, I soap and rinse again.

When bathing your pup, squeeze all the water you can from the pup's coat and apply the rinse. This kills any passengers and leaves a clean, fresh odor. Now rub the puppy as dry as you can with a towel and leave him where he will finish drying in a warm place.

If you prefer to give him a dry bath, follow directions on the container of whatever you buy. If a coarse powder is used, be sure it is thoroughly combed and brushed out before you allow the puppy his freedom. This method can clean a dog well. If you use a foaming detergent, rub it in and wipe it off thoroughly with a towel. Applying the detergent and dissolving the dirt but not removing it does no good, except to kill insects. The dirt is still on the coat, and when the pup is given his freedom he either wipes the dirt off on the rugs, furniture, or your clothes, or else it dries on him and the "bath" proves to be no bath at all.

The matter of drying is really important, especially in cold weather. Many puppy owners wash their charges in the evening, and the pups have to stay inside where it is warm to finish drying.

As puppies grow older, body odors become more pronounced. Ear canker may develop and perfume the air in the puppy's proximity with the odor of bad cheese. The pup's anal glands may become infected, and he may slide along your rugs leaving an obnoxious odor. His collar or harness may accumulate the waxy secretion from his skin and acquire the typical doggy odor.

You can bathe your pup often, but such odors remain to taunt you. However, if you treat the ear canker with what your veterinarian gives you, empty the pup's anal glands occasionally, and scrape the collar, cleansing it with alcohol and then oiling it, the pup will smell sweet and clean after a bath.

Chapter Seven

TRAINING THE YOUNG PUPPY

In a conversation with one of the greatest and most natural dog trainers in America, a man whose dogs love him and work like demons to please him, I was told this: "You can't write about training a puppy as it should be written, because if you did, no publisher would print it." He pointed to my pile of twenty books on dog training and to this present manuscript. "You've been a dog man all your life," he said. "You see thousands of dogs every year. So you know what I mean. Your book has got to be sticky with love. Train 'em with love. Always say *please* to the pup. Spoil 'em. That's what people want to read—how to spoil a pup."

This chapter, like those before it, is for the owner of a single, newly weaned pup, the owner who wants to know how to train it in elemental behavior. You can find training a wonderfully rewarding experience if you do it systematically.

HOW DOES A PUPPY LEARN?

A puppy learns through experiences that make impressions on his brain. The brain is a huge mass of nervous tissue, to and from which communications are transmitted, via nerves, much as wires carry electrical impulses. Impressions carried to the brain are received in any one of several ways. We used to speak of the five senses, but today psychologists recognize many more. However, for purposes of illustration, the puppy's *sight, taste, touch, hearing,* and *feeling* are familiar senses by which he receives impressions.

We expect that when the impression is received by our dog he will do something to indicate that he received it. If he smells a pleasant odor or appetizing food, he may show us he wants the food by begging, teasing, or even drooling. If he is sleeping and hears a noise, he may cock an ear, growl, or jump to his feet. He sees a cat run away from him and races after it. He feels the sun's heat on a warm day and pants rapidly. He tastes agreeable food, then chews and swallows it; he tastes disagreeable food and spits it out.

In short, *a dog's behavior is never uncaused.* The senses receive an impression, the nerves transmit it to the brain, and the brain transmits a response, via the nerves, to some part of the body. This almost instantaneous cycle is called a *reflex.* Briefly, reflexes are simple responses to simple stimuli. Dust in your eye causes the eye to tear. The sight of food causes saliva to flow. These are *reflexes.*

Training a dog is simply *conditioning his reflexes,* or teaching him to respond as we want him to, even though the response may be unnatural. The famous psychologist, Pavlov, was the first to show the basis for the *conditioned reflex,* as he called it. He rang a bell at the same moment he offered a dog dinner. At the sight of the food, the dog secreted saliva, which Pavlov measured. After doing this many times, Pavlov could ring the bell without offering food, and the dog would secrete saliva. By repetition and association, the dog had been trained to give the response of salivating to the stimulus of a bell's ringing.

Dogs have needs. One of the basic needs is food. Another

is the need to urinate, another to defecate. These three are especially important to all puppy owners, because the first is concerned with growth, the other two with housebreaking.

We can use the need of food in accomplishing results with a puppy at almost any time; even six or eight hours after a meal he will be hungry enough to respond to conditioning. In the case of adult dogs, it is necessary to fast the pupil thirty-six hours to have his need for food felt keenly enough to give us rapid responses and complete attention. Incidentally, some psychologists give their mature animals short rations until they have lost a quarter of their normal weight, after which they are so hungry every day that they will respond avidly; they feel a need to get back to their normal weight.

While a puppy is growing he feels the need for food, so for that very reason, puppyhood is the easiest time for us to train him.

Dogs are not born with an understanding of words, any more than human beings are. Yet some dog owners seem never to have learned this rudimentary fact. Suppose you call to an untrained puppy or dog, "Come here!" and instead he runs away. He finally returns to you of his own volition, and you vent your anger on him and possibly thrash him. The dog naturally feels that your anger was caused by his coming back. Next time he will run away farther and stay away longer when you call him.

To the dog, words are merely sounds. Give the sounds some meaning. At first, when you say "Come!", give him a tiny tidbit or give this signal only at mealtime. He will come for food. In time the word "Come!" will mean to go to you and food. After a while you can dispense with the food, as Pavlov did. Your "Come!" is equivalent to Pavlov's bell ringing.

In this way a dog can be taught to respond to different

words, and under a patient trainer he will learn quickly. Your family dog can easily be taught to understand the meaning of two hundred words—and even four hundred is not impossible.

Words are not the only signals that can be used. Shepherds teach their dogs to respond to gestures or whistles. You can teach your dog to look when you snap your fingers or clap and then go to the place where you point. Your feet also make excellent indicators for wordless commands. A dog looks at your feet more naturally than at your hands. Some of the best trainers use their feet to point with.

Two toots of a whistle, for instance, can mean one desired action, one toot "Attention," three toots something else, a long blast still another action. Hunters use horns both to cheer their hounds on and to call them in.

All training is a matter of habit formation. Some actions may require dozens of repetitions to be well learned. Mistakes and lapses are bound to occur. So remember this: *don't start to train your dog to do any specific action unless you're prepared to complete the job.*

As you progress, try diligently never to let a slip or exception occur. Be firm. "The greatest firmness is the greatest mercy." The dog is your vassal; he must respect your laws.

A puppy's attention darts from one object of interest to another. Therefore the first requirement in education is to capture his attention. You can't do this as well when his stomach is full and his inclination is to sleep as you can when he is hungry. All of the first part of your puppy training must be of the simplest nature, and your best ally is hunger—moderate hunger, of course (not that hunger is painful), because you want your pup to grow, but enough hunger to keep him keen and attentive. When he is nearly grown, longer fast periods—

twenty-four hours or even thirty-six, as I said, may help him to be attentive.

Some trainers will tell you that all you need to do is to repeat and pet; "petting is all the reward the puppy needs." But psychologists laugh, knowing that tidbits of a more substantial nature are what bring the quick results.

In the future you will hear, more and more, the terms *conditioning* and *reinforcements*. These will replace the words *training* and *rewards*. If the change seems to you to be much ado about nothing, you should understand the reasons behind the change.

A *reward* is a prize, a *reinforcement* is like a brick in a wall that you are erecting. Each tidbit you use properly, builds the wall. You can't erect it all at once, with one big brick or casting because the nervous mechanism isn't of such a nature. You can tumble the wall down all at once, or at least more easily than you erected it. This process of knocking the wall down is called brainwashing by laymen (who usually do not understand the term) or *de-conditioning* or *extinguishing* by psychologists.

Conditioning is a gradual process established brick by brick (each brick is a correct response to a signal). So from here on we shall not say *training*, but *conditioning*. We'll not talk about *rewards* but about *reinforcements*.

Reinforcements

What are the best tidbits to use? Anything convenient for you to handle that the puppy loves to eat. When I train I use pieces of frankfurter cut about an inch long. Or sliced liver boiled and cut into one-half or three-quarter inch squares. Almost any hungry puppy will respond instantly to liver. I let the dog nibble each piece from my fingers; I do not let him swallow it in a gulp.

Pieces of coarse kibbled dog biscuit are often used, pieces of "dog candy," which is sold under several trade names, or pellets made from dry dog food. Some pups respond to fried bacon or salt pork better than to any other food stimulus. One important research into dog psychology was conducted using only one-inch-long pieces of fried crisp bacon.

The tone of one's voice can convey approval, too, but not to the extent that so many persons seem to think. "Nice doggy" is about all the average puppy hears most of his life.

Petting is also reinforcing, but the pup must first have been handled a great deal and have grown accustomed to your hands. Patting a dog on the head is practiced only by those ignorant of dogs. Watch an old-timer who has a way with dogs learned from long association. His hand never comes down over the dog's head, but up or sideways and ends by taking hold of the dog's ear and gently rubbing it, or rubbing under the throat—always beside or under the chin or head. To condition a puppy, one should not attempt to pet one that does not already know the comfort and pleasure a hand can be.

Compared with tasty tidbits, petting is an inefficient reinforcement. The term *brainwashing,* which we so often hear used, is usually precisely the opposite of what most people think it means. We hear that an expatriate from a Western nation went to a Communist nation and was brainwashed into their ideology. Not so; he was *conditioned.* True brainwashing is usually a terrifying experience or else a long, slow process.

Negative reinforcements

Where most people use the term punishment, we substitute *negative reinforcement.* This is a form of brainwashing. When we observe misbehavior in a dog and want to eradicate it, we apply a distasteful reaction to the puppy's action. This is usually done by tearing down the bricks in the wrong kind of wall that has been built up in the puppy's brain. It is possible to reinforce negatively very violently or painfully which will end the undesirable reaction all at once. If a puppy jumps on an electric stove whose grills are red hot, his foot or feet become badly burned, and he is cured of jumping on the stove. If he chews on an electric wire and gets a severe shock, he usually shuns even strings. The more severe the pain received, the quicker the de-conditioning.

Something that actually hurts the puppy is the best de-conditioner. Something that, while not hurting, gives the puppy a proper idea of who is boss, is the next best. Some action that frightens him is only fair and in many ways inferior. What looks like de-conditioning, but which neither hurts nor frightens, may be actually conditioning your puppy to misbehave. Threatening only makes him give you the dog laugh; it's not conditioning at all.

It is actually a kindness to de-condition a puppy if it is necessary. The unconditioned pup becomes obnoxious to others, who usually show it by their actions toward him. As he grows older you must restrict his activity, or he may be kicked around by the neighbors or even stoned. In the long run it is crueler not to cure a dog of improper responses than to de-condition him when he needs it. And the best de-conditioner is that which makes the dog recognize that he has brought this on himself by his own action.

The way to look at it is to ask yourself how does a dog learn not to do things in nature. Watch a mother dog teaching her puppies. She may be eating and growls when a puppy comes near the food. The growl corresponds to Pavlov's bell ringing. The puppy has smelled the food and gone to it. He hears a growl. He pays no attention to it the first time. Then *wham!* He feels his mother's teeth snap at him, feels himself thrown through the air, and feels the blow when he slams against some object or lands on the ground. He gets a good lesson—and a natural lesson—and that one lesson is usually all he needs to know that a growl means to *stay away*.

Whatever method of persuasion is used, the time-lag between the misdeed and the pain must be as short as possible. Ideally it should be instantaneous, a lag equivalent to touching the hot coal and feeling the pain. If you wait much longer, the puppy's attention may be focused on something else, and he may feel he is being punished for something entirely different.

With this introduction, we may consider what means serve our purpose best.

The Open Hand. In the case of little puppies a smart slap is about as easy and effective as you need. It must hurt, but it usually hurts the trainer, especially if she is a woman. With older dogs few women slap hard enough. In personal discussions I have often brought in a large hound puppy and asked the woman with whom I was discussing the subject to slap the pup on the side—hard. Very few women have ever slapped hard enough to make the pup realize he was being punished. The pup's wagging tail indicated he thought he was being petted.

If anyone slaps the puppy, and the little tyke fights back, then obviously he has not received more than an annoyance, and the puppy is actually being trained to be vicious.

The Rolled Newspaper. This frequently recommended method of punishment is effective if the pup is swatted hard enough to hurt him and not simply to frighten him. It takes quite a blow to accomplish this purpose, and a lot of taps simply make him afraid of you and not conscious that he is being disciplined. You may have read that slapping a pup makes him hand-shy and that you should use a rolled-up newspaper. This is simply not true. The hand that slaps his cheek will have been used to feed him and will again be reinforcing a correct response, and the pup soon learns that the hand can be put to both uses. He sees your hand holding his food pan at feeding time too. The rolled-up newspaper isn't always handy whenever you are with the pup, but your hand is always there. The application of treatment, as we have seen, must be instantaneous.

The Switch. Whether we think it humane or not, thousands of puppies are effectively de-conditioned by switching. Nearly all hunters resort to this method, and they switch hard, not chasing after the pup, making it afraid of them, but picking it up by the scruff of the neck and really hurting. And those puppies, results show, actually love their masters more than do the puppies conditioned by letting them have their own way with slight discipline.

The Voice. There is no doubt that a sharp command or a scolding tone will accomplish something in disciplining a dog, but it produces such an effect only if the animal has first been taught the meaning of the words you use. Emphasis given to any signal gets a quicker or surer reaction. Tone alone can be used to frighten in some instances—as, for example, if a puppy is getting ready to defecate where he should not and you turn loose a loud barrage of words.

Shaking. Some of the most adept and successful conditioners pick up a puppy and shake him vigorously for punishment. This is one of the most effective methods. No pain is inflicted, the pup learns of your strength and gains respect for you, and because you have kept hold of him when the shaking is over, he recognizes that you are firm and just.

The Use of Water. Being wet in summer won't harm your outdoor puppy, and the use of water can serve as an effective measure. Even a water pistol squirted in his face, a bucket of cold water dashed over a large pup when he is tied to his kennel, a thorough dunking in a tub of water, are all ways in which water can be used effectively.

The Dark Closet. When the puppy misbehaves you can put him into a dark closet where he will be lonesome. It must be done quickly, with as little time as possible elapsing between his wrong act and your picking him up and rushing him to the closet.

The Broom. No more natural tool for training can be put into the hands of a woman than a broom, and yet how few ever think of using one. A few swishes of a new broom over a young pup is often magic. If a pup fights it, then an old broom is called for. One woman client of ours had an especially obstreperous barking mongrel yearling pup that she couldn't control. It was really too large and strong for her anyway. I suggested she chain it to the radiator pipe and use a broom for training. In one afternoon, by saying "be still" and walloping it with a worn-out broom, she had it perfectly trained. But I happen to know she broke the kitchen overhead light, so she must have taken some hefty swings. "Made me feel so good to realize I could wallop the bark out of that mutt after all the insults I took from him in the past," she told me. "But best of all, he's now the best-behaved dog in our neighborhood. Minds and loves us all—even me."

Satiation. For those hunters who read this book I must mention the satiating method of punishment. It is based on the fact that any animal can get too much of a good thing. Let us suppose that you have a beagle that persists in running on fox tracks as well as those of rabbits. You live in the country. Often you have to drive several miles to retrieve your puppy from a person to whose house he has gone, tired and lame.

There are several suppliers who sell scents of various mammals extracted in liquid form. I have broken many dogs this way. The scent may be sprayed on the pup from a small atomizer, but a better way, I think, is to push some cotton into the toe of an old stocking. Pour the scent on the lump, and every day smack the pup about the head with the lump. He has to live in the odor for a week or more and gets so sick of it that when he gets loose from his chain he wants no more of it and leaves the foxes alone.

TEACHING RESPONSES

Following are some of the useful signals to which every puppy should be taught to respond, and suggestions for training your puppy to obey. I suggest you be original in the commands (signals) you use. The instructors of classes in dog training emphasize the use of the same words for everybody's dogs, and there is value in this idea, especially when the dog changes hands, because the new owner can use the same signals as the first and does not need to familiarize himself with new words. However, my experience leads me to believe that no two persons pronounce the same word with the same inflection, so the dog may not respond to even the same words that he was taught. If you say "applesauce" when you want your pup to shake hands, and teach him to respond to that word, it is more fun than saying "shake hands." He has no hands, and he doesn't shake anyway, but simply lifts his foreleg and extends it. You can even say "sit" when you want him to stand up.

The point is: decide what words to use for signals for the desired responses, and use them and no others. Let an early lesson be—the meaning of "no."

Meaning of "no"

It is so easy to teach this most useful of all word signals! When the pup is hungry, place a large bone—too large to be swallowed—on the floor. When the puppy takes it, which of course he will, slap his face with your open hand and say "No!" Let there be no other conversation. He will soon be back at the luscious treat, and each time he tries it he hears "No!" and gets slapped. It is amazing how quickly he learns. Soon you can stand across the room from him, say "No!" and he will heed the word.

Now you must teach him what "take it" means. Or perhaps you prefer "all right" or "yours"; any short terse expression to indicate to him it is all right to take the food. You may practically have to put the previously forbidden food in his mouth to show him what the positive command means. With a little persistence you can drop a small piece of food, say "no," and after he has stared longingly at it, say "take it," and he will respond.

These signals are especially useful at feeding time. Larger puppies, in their eagerness to eat, often hook their chins over a bowl of food the owner is placing on the floor and tip it over. The word "no" puts an end to such bad manners.

Having shown him the meaning of "no" is applied to not touching food, you must extend it to other activities. If the pup starts chewing on your bedroom slipper, say "no." If he does not stop, take it away and slap him with it.

If he jumps on furniture, you can easily teach him the consequences. Say "no," and if he does not jump down, you can slap him, shake him, or switch him and put him on the floor. In no time he learns that jumping on furniture is practically a request for you to punish him; he brings it on himself.

If he chews your rug or linoleum, say "no" as you punish him, catching him in the act if possible.

If he nips your ankles, performs the sexual act, as puppies are wont to, on your children's legs, say "no" and punish him.

In a short time he will learn what you mean when he hears
"no."

Scolding. The word "no" may be said with so much emphasis that it may be almost used as discipline, but only after
you have conditioned your pup to know what it means. And
when the puppy knows that "no" means to stop doing whatever he is doing, and is not obeying, a torrent of "no's" fired
at him will often produce a quick result. Many puppies soon
learn that your tone of voice in saying "no" so emphatically,
when used with other words, means the same thing. Then it
becomes scolding.

"Shake," "sit," "lie down"

Use the reinforcement method to condition your dog to
obey these word signals. First place an old table against the
wall. This makes it unnecessary for you to get down on the
floor, and besides that, you can teach the pup these signals
better on a table.

Put a harness on the dog, place him on the table, and restrain him with a leash attached to the wall behind him so
that his chest is even with the front edge of the table. Let him
smell the tiny tidbit. He will be eager for it and put out a paw.
At this instant, say "Shake!" or whatever word you have
chosen, and, holding the reward in your fingers, let him nibble
it. When it is gone, pause a minute and say "Shake!"—one
word, not a sentence—again. You'll be amazed at how quickly
he will learn what the word means. Repeat the reaction twenty
times for two or three sessions, until he always sticks out a
paw when he hears the sound "Shake!" He has then mastered
the lesson. Don't forget to show your approval when he
performs properly; make your response immediate and en-
thusiastic.

After a few sessions teach him to lie down and to stand up.

These are easy, because you can hold the tidbit slightly below the table top and the dog will have to lie down to reach it. When he is down let him nibble the reward. Hold the reward high and say "Stand up." Up he gets, and you feed him.

The next signal can be "Sit!" The old method of forcing a puppy to sit by pushing his hind parts down while his head is pulled up by a leash is effective but time-consuming. It is much easier to simply attach your puppy's leash to a tree and stand in front of him. He will soon become sick of standing and sit down. Say "sit" and immediately slip him his tidbit. Take a step backward, and he will rise on all fours. Step toward him again and wait until he sits and give him a tidbit. He will seem to catch on all at once. Repeat the lessons daily until he never fails to sit when he hears the word.

Once you have partially established these habits, say "sit" when the pup is loose in the house, and show your approval each time he responds properly.

Training to "come!"

More puppy owners fail in this phase of conditioning than in any other. It is almost impossible to *force* a pup to come to you, but it is easy to coax him to respond by using tidbits.

Teach this command when the pup is hungry. Tie a light, strong cord (heavy fishline is good) to his collar and be sure the collar is tight, so that it won't slip over his head. Take him to a familiar area and, holding the leash, let him stray away. Then attract him by calling "Come here!" (or "Come!"). Always use the same word or words. When he comes, let him nibble a tidbit from your fingers. Repeat this about a dozen times. Next day take him out again, but this time use a longer cord and go to an unfamiliar area, where strange sights allure him. If he doesn't respond at once when you call him, remind him by lightly jerking the cord. Do it twenty times, at least.

Try him, perhaps a day later, in the familiar area without a cord. He soon will form the habit of coming when you call. But remember this, during the training period, never call the dog unless you feel fairly certain he will respond. If he has started racing after a car, don't call him and expect him to come to you. Only when the habit has been fully established will he come each time he is called.

Teaching for "go bed," "stay," and "wait"

When your puppy is very young, just putting him on his bed or leading him to it and saying "bed" as you do soon gets him to know what "bed" means. But this doesn't always work so, to get him to react to the word bed, drop a tidbit into the bed as he is looking, and *as he jumps in* say *bed*. Take him out or call him to come and drop another tidbit. Keep up the action and reinforcement twenty times and twenty times the next day when he is hungry.

As the pup grows older send him to his bed and say "stay" or "wait." Take a broom, and when he comes away before you call him, chase him back, swatting his rear end with the broom. Make the interval between your sending him to his bed and your call to come longer and longer and feed him a tidbit. Give another tidbit for staying in his bed. Occasionally, while he is there, take him a tidbit, and as you give it to him say "stay" or "wait." Go out of the room, leaving him on his bed.

This conditioning accustoms him to being alone, and you will have a much better dog as a result.

If your puppy knows to go to his bed and stay until you call him to come, making him first sit and then stay is a simple matter. Place him in a new situation and try him. If you have not already trained him to understand what "stay" means, make him sit and back away from him, saying "stay" distinctly. At the first sign of movement say "no, stay." If he does not catch on quickly, put a screw eye and pulley in the wall, or in a tree or post, depending on where you are training him. Place it as high from the ground as the pup is tall. Run a long, strong cord from his collar through the pulley and back along his side to your hand. If he leaves his spot before you say "come," haul him back with the cord. When you say "come," slacken the cord and let him trot to you. Give him the tidbit.

Training to "heel"

Shepherd dogs are natural heel drivers. Dalmatians naturally run behind the heels of horses. Not very long ago a dog conditioned to heel "dogged one's footsteps"—he really heeled. Very few people train dogs to heel any more. And now the obedience classes train dogs to walk at the owner's left side when they say "heel"—a rather ridiculous notion, when it is just as easy to say "side" or "at side."

Why not use the sensible words "at side?" If, however, you want to exhibit your pup in competition, the judge will expect you to say "heel" when you want the dog to walk at your side.

You can most easily train your dog to walk wherever you want him by using a little switch and a short leash. Let him walk beside you while you hold his leash in your left hand and keep admonishing him "at side." When he pulls ahead of you, snap him across the nose and pull him back. When he walks with the leash loose, dole out a tidbit now and then. It's only a matter of repetition, and soon you will find he will walk along well and on no leash at all. If you own an electric trainer, you can harness him with it, and instead of the switch, shock him ever so lightly when he pulls too strongly.

LEASH BREAKING

Put a collar or harness on your pup at as early an age as you wish. He probably won't object to it. Flat collars are usually used on puppies with short hair (beagles, Dalmatians, pointers, et cetera), and round collars on bushy- or long-haired pups (collies, German shepherds). Choke collars are particularly useful for dogs which are difficult to manage. When using one, it is necessary to jerk on the leash, then release quickly. If you use one on your dog, be sure the chain slips freely through the ring. The kind of leash you use is of great importance. A smooth chain with a leather handle is best. If you use a leather leash, the puppy soon learns that he can chew it in half and will try to chew any leash thereafter. Even when you are walking with your pup he may keep trying to chew on the leash. With a chain leash you can tie him up and not be afraid of losing him.

After your pup is leash-broken it makes little difference which you use, but a harness is easier on the puppy when you go for a walk.

A leash and collar are always used for training, never a harness. A harness permits the puppy to tug and lean, and results in a badly trained dog.

Some trainers believe that snapping a leash to a puppy's collar and letting him drag it about the house is a good way to begin leash training. It does no harm, but many puppies soon find the leash is a toy and chew on it, which is not your purpose in attaching it.

Breaking to a leash can be done by fastening the leash's snap to the collar or harness, holding the handle, and letting the puppy learn that he can't get away. Some trainers fasten the leash to a tree or a stake and let the pup struggle until he learns it's no use and becomes resigned to it. But it is better if you hold the leash yourself. This requires but a few minutes' time and is much easier on the puppy.

To make him walk on the leash, coax him, don't drag him. Train him when he is hungry, and carry some small rewards that you can give him as you two walk along together.

Don't lose your temper. One's natural inclination is to pull and drag the pup if he holds back, with feet braced. That will not make him move ahead, but coaxing will.

When he is very young you can teach him not to tug on the leash, because he is so easily jerked backward if he pulls too hard. Don't reach out when he comes to the end of the leash, to ease the pressure on his neck; that teaches him to lunge and tug. Rather, set yourself and let him learn that he can upset himself if he lunges.

HOUSEBREAKING

Housebreaking is obviously one of the first conditioning tasks that face any dog owner. It calls for patience and alertness. The key to successful and quick housebreaking is to anticipate when a dog should go out and, at such times, to take him out without fail. From the beginning establish a routine. Take the puppy outdoors immediately after each meal and as often as possible between meals, including early morning and late evening walks. This is a total of six to eight times during twenty-four hours. When the dog voids outdoors, pet him, speak in a kind voice, and show real approval. This will make him understand he has behaved well.

Conversely, show real disapproval when you catch him voiding or getting ready to void indoors. Speak angrily. Let there be no doubt of your disapproval. However, it is of little use to discipline a dog after he has voided; he won't understand why he is being punished.

Alertness on your part can greatly shorten the time required to housebreak a dog. If you see him squatting to void, say "no" and make a loud noise. This startles and interrupts him. Take him outdoors immediately. You can hardly demonstrate your wishes more clearly.

If you are not attentive during this period, if you allow your dog to remain indoors for long periods of time, if you do not show consistent approval when he behaves well and clear disapproval when he does not, you will merely confuse him and decrease the effectiveness of your efforts.

The paper method of housebreaking, recently developed and tried with definite success, is worth the attention of the dog owners who have enough spare room at home to allow a clutter of newspapers to remain on the floor for the time it takes to condition a puppy.

The method is based on the theory that a puppy first learns to void in response to his mother's lapping. When his mother no longer guides him in his natural function, his next stimulation is *feeling* via his feet; he *feels* for familiar ground. For example, if your puppy was reared on a short-cropped lawn, you may be certain that he will seek out a rug with a high nap, because it *feels* most like lawn under his feet. A puppy used to sawdust will search for a soft, uneven surface. And a puppy who is used to newspaper will void when he *feels* newspaper under his feet.

The first step in this method of housebreaking is to get the puppy used to being on newspaper. For several days keep him on a floor that is covered with newspaper. After that leave a wide expanse of newspaper in a room, so that the puppy can find it and use it. When, by repetition, the habit is established, you can place only one sheet of newspaper on the floor.

The next step is to move the paper close to the door and let him use it there for several days or weeks. Then move it just outside the door, with one edge showing inside. He can't get to it and will whine to go out. You must be alert during this crucial time and open the door immediately; after he has voided, show your approval.

Then move the paper to the area where you want him to void. After a while reduce the size of the paper each time he goes outdoors until he associates the place, instead of the paper, with what is expected of him. Then he is completely housebroken. Punish him for mistakes after you feel he really knows what he should do.

The apartment-house puppy is often taught to use a newspaper in a corner of the kitchen or bathroom. The paper is rolled up and discarded and replaced by a new one. Some puppies are put out in courts or taken for walks along the curb and in time learn to prefer the curb or dirt in the court to newspaper.

A good way to housebreak a puppy four months old or older is based on the fact that all puppies tend not to soil their own beds. Make a flat box for his bed, having the box perhaps six or eight inches high and as square as the puppy is long— no larger. Put a pad or old carpet in the bottom. Obtain a short chain with two swivels in it. Screw an eyebolt into the wall a foot above the floor of the box and hook the chain to this eyebolt. The chain should be just long enough to reach to within six inches of the outer edge of the box. Snap the outer end of the chain to the puppy's collar and let this constitute his quarters whenever you must leave him alone.

Put the pup out or take him for a walk as late as possible at night, and again as early in the morning as possible. When you are with him let him loose and watch him. At the first sign of squatting motions indicative of elimination, call "No, no" in your most severe tone and carry him out, or to his paper if you live where he must defecate in the apartment.

I have known this method to be effective with even younger puppies. By the time the pup has outgrown the original bed he needs no chain at night; he is well housebroken.

If you live in the North, it may take a day or two to get the puppy to eliminate on the first snow of the season. Even though he is used to going outdoors, the snow feels so different to his touch that he has to be left out until he has completed his task and encouraged as he does so.

You may wonder why I have not mentioned the old house-breaking methods of rubbing the pup's nose in his feces when he defecates in the wrong place or of taking him to such a spot and slapping him. This is precisely the wrong way to train. A puppy's brain is not capable of reasoning—I soiled in the living room when I should have soiled on the paper in the kitchen; now I'm being punished for it.

There are now available synthetic odors which both repel and attract. The repelling kind is to be sprayed on spots where your pup or another dog has soiled. The urine smell is supposed to be neutralized by it, and the new odor becomes repellent.

The attractive odor is used to spray a place where you want your puppy to eliminate. This works better in the case of older pups and mature dogs. A puppy is almost full grown before he becomes interested in the urine of older dogs. I would say it is the time when a male starts lifting his leg. Just the smell of another dog's urine evokes a reflex which almost impels him to urinate over the odor left by the previous dog.

STAIRS

Every puppy must learn to walk downstairs. Climbing stairs is easy, although quite an achievement for a small puppy. Try to put yourself in the puppy's place, then you will realize how large a single step is, what a climb it is proportionately to the size of the dog. Let him tumble down a flight once, and the achievement of going down becomes all the greater. In the case of young pups of small breeds, jumping down one step is jumping from a height twice as tall as the puppy.

So to stair-break your pup put him on the first step and let him jump down by enticing him, then the second step and, when he can do that, the third step. But be patient until he is old enough and large enough for you to start to stair-break him, and then use tidbits. If he is afraid to come down three steps, he is probably too young for the training.

BREAKING THE PUP OF CARSICKNESS

When you take your puppy for his very first ride you will probably learn whether you have a naturally carsick pet. Some pups are never carsick; others vomit before they have traveled one hundred yards. Some merely slobber without vomiting. But even this is a nuisance and calls for some preventative.

Part of the cause of carsickness is fright and part is motion sickness. It is easy to get a pup accustomed to a car by taking him in it while the car is standing still and holding him on your lap. If he is small, spread paper on the floor and feed him on it. Or, if you have a carrier, set it inside the car with your pet in the carrier, start the motor, and leave him there for ten minutes. Do this every day for a week.

If it is motion sickness that causes vomiting, your veterinarian will gladly supply you with drugs such as Dramamine, and a combination of atropine (or Metropine) with phenobarbital will dry the secretions and quiet the pup. Usually giving small doses of Nembutal (sodium pentabarbital), Amytal, or phenobarbital, fifteen minutes before starting out, will accomplish the desired effect.

QUIETING A NOISY PUP

A noisy dog is generally a nuisance, yet it isn't difficult to stop needless barking. Simply show your disapproval and punish him. Be sure to allow no exceptions.

Some pups understand only severe treatment. When this becomes necessary, the following measures may be taken. In summer, water can be sloshed over a pup tied to a kennel. If you use this method, fill the container again immediately after the lesson and set it where he can see it. When he barks again, come rushing out and slosh him again. Repeat it as often as necessary to establish in his mind the fact that barking is to all intents calling you to come and slosh him. If you have a long garden hose and can lay it out along the ground to your puppy's house, you can arrange a sprayer which is most efficient in curing the barking habit. Mount the nozzle on a stick driven into the ground so that it is aimed directly at the dog. The other end of the hose is, of course, connected with a faucet inside or outside your house. When the puppy barks, simply turn on the faucet. When he stops, turn it off again. This method is excellent in warm weather on larger puppies.

I showed a friend how to cure a grown cocker spaniel by having a tub made by sawing a barrel in half and filling the tub with water after it had been set up close to the dog. This was a dog which kept all the neighbors awake nights. The kennel was set where many neighbors could see and hear, so my friend felt that people would call him inhumane if he used a switch.

One Sunday he devoted the whole day to discipline. Each time the dog barked, he rushed out, yelling "Be still!", hauled the dog out of the doghouse into which he retreated when he saw his master coming, plunked him down into the tub of water, and let him scramble out and ignominiously shake and crawl into his house.

By the third dowsing neighbors were at the windows applauding. By 2 P.M. the dog was cured, so that all my friend needs to do is say "Be still!" and silence reigns.

Some large puppies can't be cured by any means other than physical pain. You may find yourself faced with a choice of either disposing of the pup or using a whip. But this is almost never the case with little puppies.

Suppose the pup must be left alone indoors. As you know, there are dogs that will howl or bark incessantly when the family goes out. Some grown dogs will vent their frustrations at being left by chewing furniture, tearing couch pillows to bits, or in other ways. All of this unsocial behavior was conditioned into the pup. It may have started by him seeing you leave and whining to go with you. He kept up the whining until it became a bark, and you soon returned. He learned that the barking brought you back. So next time you went he barked again, and you returned. He learned how to make you return.

Dogs are persistent. Some of my coon dogs, trained to "bark tree," will find a tree up which a raccoon has climbed and sit at the foot barking all night if I can't find them.

To untrain a puppy which barks at being left home, you must spend some time. Go out and leave him alone while you sit outside where you can hear him, but where he can't see, smell, or hear you. At the first sign of barking, rush in and show him that he called you back but to punish him.

Repeat the lesson, letting longer and longer periods of time elapse, until you feel sure that no matter how long you are away he will not bark.

Puppies which are quiet when left alone seldom become destructive when they are grown. It is the dog that has learned to get his own way that becomes furious when he finds he is balked, and proceeds to tear furniture or chew holes in doors.

Just as dispositions can be kept sound by what you do around your puppy's food pan, so a sound temperament can be established by making a puppy understand that he can't have your close companionship all the time. Kennel dogs exist without a human being close to them for nine-tenths of every day. Your being in the house does not need to mean to your dog that he must be with you. And that is where training comes in. What's more, you can teach him what the words *wait* or *stay* mean better at this time than at any other (see page 197).

TRAINING AGAINST JUMPING-UP

No one, especially a guest in your home, appreciates a puppy jumping on him without an invitation. The small pup who jumps on people in the house may appear affectionate to members of his family, but remember that when he is a grown dog he will do the same thing in the muddy street and will be considered a nuisance. The best method of training is by means of a painful procedure that at the same time lets him think he is bringing the pain on himself. When he stands up, rub his ear but step *lightly* on his hind toes, so that he can't see you doing it. He thinks that jumping up gives him a pain in his toes, and soon he won't repeat it. All the members of the household must cooperate in his training in order for it to be completely successful.

THE BITING HABIT

Very few people want a dog that bites. Fortunately it is not impossible to cure the biting habit. In the case of the pup that bites mischievously, an instantaneous slap across the face of the puppy as he bites, and a sharp "no," cures it. However, a young pup that snaps constantly may not be worth training. One reason why we have such reliable dogs today is that their originators knew enough to destroy every unreliable pup before it had a chance to breed. There are too many pups with inherently wonderful dispositions for anyone to waste time on a mean one. It is true that mean dogs can often be cured, but such dogs will sometimes bite with very little provocation in later years.

Some trainers advise us never to disturb a dog when he is eating. I am sure they are wrong. You can condition a puppy to be vicious by letting him think his food is sacred. There is no better way to insure a sound disposition than training while feeding. I have always seen to it that I can reach right into any of my dogs' feeding pans without being bitten. As puppies are growing it is well to make a practice of showing them you will not stand for growling. Take the food away and pet them when you do. Cover your pup's food pan with your hand and at the least show of temper scold him and, if necessary, slap his face. But never taunt him or tease him with the food. Once your puppy gets the idea that he doesn't need to protect his food, that there's plenty for him, and he can rely on it, you have helped to insure a sound disposition.

OVERCOMING NOISE SHYNESS

Puppies that are noise-shy—or gun-shy, as it is sometimes called—may come by the trait through inheritance, but with many more it is acquired. Such a puppy presents a special problem to the owner who plans to raise him as a hunting dog.

Thousands of dogs become almost sick with fear during thunderstorms. Many city dogs cringe at the sound of traffic. And on the Fourth of July, in those places where fireworks are still permitted, the poor noise-shy dogs will be found hidden in closets or under beds, quivering from fright.

It is easy to condition a pup, which is slightly edgy by nature, to be afraid of noise. If you tiptoe around him for fear of making noises that will disturb him, you are extremely likely to have a noise-shy animal. Loud noises will be terrifying to him from his earliest recollection. Experience shows that much handling from the start and plenty of noise associated with pleasant experiences tend to produce a sound puppy. One kennel owner of my acquaintance made a point of creating a lot of noise at feeding time. He could be heard a city block away, banging boards on the roofs of doghouses or slamming the dogs' feeding pans. Even the youngest puppy learned to associate a lot of noise with something he liked—food. This breeder's pointers were never afraid of gunshot sounds.

THE PIDDLING PUP

Because of sloppy breeding—lack of selection—many puppies have weak bladder sphincter muscles. A sphincter is a circular muscle that in this case circles the neck of the bladder and holds the urine back. Weakness in the muscle is inherited, as is the tendency to relax tension on it at either joy or fright.

This fact is most important in puppy training. Few persons want a piddling puppy. Male piddlers will often squirt urine a considerable distance, and when one jumps up on a person likely as not he will sprinkle trousers or stockings. The female or male that squats down and leaves a small pond on the floor, which he or she then proceeds to step in and track about the house, is actually too obnoxious to keep. Yet once propinquity has endeared the pup to the family they may keep a mop beside the front door, where most of the piddling occurs, rather than try to train the pup or get a new one.

Piddling usually starts by a puppy with a naturally weak sphincter cowering beneath a huge human figure. Imagine the positions reversed. You are the pup. You look up at this gigantic man or woman perhaps thirty or forty times as large as you. You are frightened; you are in a new situation. Fright loosens even brave dogs' sphincters; is it any wonder it relaxes the little puppy's?

To attempt to check this trouble, or at least to prevent its becoming a habit, never bend down over a pup. Squat down before it all you want, or kneel down, but never bend over it. If you have to pick up the puppy, do so by making him come to you. Do not chase him and frighten him, because every time you do you are strengthening the piddling habit.

As early as possible after you have trained the pup to sit, make him sit before you every time he approaches—not cringe, but sit. This helps a great deal to break him of piddling. A sitting pup has difficulty piddling; and he will not have the inclination, because his mind is on the food he is sitting to get.

KEEPING THE PUP OFF FURNITURE

You yourself may have trained the puppy to jump on furniture. You surely did if you let him sit on your lap. It comes down to a choice of never letting him sit on your lap or letting him and perhaps giving him a chair of his own that he is conditioned to use. Even this is difficult to train him to accept if you ever sit on another chair with the dog in your lap.

You can keep your puppy from climbing on furniture by making it an unpleasant experience for him. Push tacks through stiff cardboard, cover them with a cloth, and place the cardboard on the furniture.

If you or members of your family are forgetful, this might

also become an unpleasant experience for you. You may therefore prefer to sprinkle the furniture with powder the odor of
which is obnoxious to the dog but which is not noticeable to
humans. Be sure to brush or vacuum-clean the furniture after
the training period is over. If your pup chews on the furniture,
reprimand him. If this does not work, paint ipecac, tabasco
sauce, cayenne pepper, capsicum, quinine, or pennyroyal
where he is likely to chew.

These repellents constitute a form of de-conditioning. Your
puppy learns habits from them as he does from your words.
When you are present you can, of course, speak to him and
make him obey. Use the word "no," "off," or "down," or just
give vent to a lot of "no's" in a tone he can't fail to understand even if he doesn't know the words.

WATCHDOG CONDITIONING

It is much easier to condition a puppy to bark than to train
him not to bark. A watchdog must be alert for unusual sounds.
He should be better than any door bell and alert you even when
steps are heard in your apartment hall, or coming up the front
walk if you live in suburbs or the country. You may want him
to bark when a car drives into your driveway or yard.

I like the effect of the words "What's that?" pronounced so
they sound to the dog "wazzat?" There is a hissing sound to
this, and dogs respond well to it. When the house is quiet, and
you and the pup are sitting at ease, have a confederate make
some unusual noise outside, perhaps push up a window, or
scuffle in the hall, or cough, or make a strange noise with his
voice. Jump up startled and say "Wazzat?" You'll be amazed
how you communicate your feigned state of mind to your pup.
As you rush to the place where the sound originated he will
run there too, usually expressing his startled attitude by bark-

ing. Reinforce his response with a tidbit. Repeat until you have him barking as much as you want—enough to give alarm, but not too much alarm.

HUNTING DOG TRAINING

Dogs have such strongly inherited behavior patterns—or mental aptitudes, as some call them—that future hunting dogs need very little training for their appointed tasks while they are still young puppies. All such pups can do well when familiarized with the environment in which they will someday work. Bird dogs and hounds need to know the woods and fields; retrievers learn the fun of swimming, guard dogs the ways of people, greyhounds the wide open spaces. Best of all, such early education gets their owners out in the open—an additional advantage from owning a dog.

CAR AND BICYCLE CHASING

It is quite rare for puppies to chase cars since that tendency seems to come at an age when the herding and protective behavior patterns appear in the dog's development. However, a word here is nevertheless appropriate because this tendency may manifest itself during late puppyhood, and that is the time to squelch this behavior. Once the aptitude becomes a habit, it is much harder to stop. At the first sign of it, scold your pup. If scolding—"No, no, no, no, no," in your harshest tones —won't stop it, then get several neighbors to give you rides in their cars. Leave the pup running loose with a ten-foot leash attached to his collar. When your friend drives by with you in the car and your pup comes out and barks, have the friend stop the car quickly. This will surprise your pup, who up to now has gathered the impression that cars are afraid of him, his ego growing with each car he chased away. You will deflate his ego by jumping out and stepping on the lead and chastising him. If you do this three times, he will learn that all cars are not afraid of him and that you may be in one.

There are many other ways to stop car chasing. Emptying half a bucket of water on the dog, throwing Fourth-of-July caps done up with gravel in a little paper bomb in front of the dog, using a long, light lead from the side of the road and upsetting him when he reaches the end of it—these are all helpful. But riding in the car and punishing the pup cures the unwanted behavior most quickly.

No one likes a dog to run along beside his bicycle, barking at it. Even worse, some tragic accidents have been caused in this manner. The same principles apply in stopping the habit as in breaking the car-chasing habit. Scolding from the side lines sometimes helps. Using a long, light lead to upset him and having the rider squirt water from a large water pistol into his face are other ways of stopping the habit. But again, puppies are less likely to chase bicycles than are older dogs. Try to end the tendency with the first few attempts.

SIMPLE TRICKS

Teaching little responses is a matter of repetition and of always giving the same signal. One simple way to teach a desired response in the form of a "trick" is to wait until the dog is about to do something spontaneous, then give the signal, feed him the reinforcement, and pet him.

In one evening I trained a hunting hound to do three useful tricks—"Go round back," "Get on the table," and "Get on the chair." When I let him out at night he usually came to the front

214 HOW TO SELECT, TRAIN, AND BREED YOUR DOG

door because it was convenient to put him out that way. On one occasion when he returned and barked, I poked my head out and said, "Go round back." Then I went to the back door, whistled, and let him in. It was amazing to me how quickly he learned the response.

To teach him the second trick I took him into the cellar and placed him on a table where I brushed him. He loved to be scrubbed with a hard brush, so I thought it would be an adequate reinforcer. I said, "Jump on the table." He soon caught on that he got his brushing when he complied. Then I shifted to the chair and brushed him on that. He learned what "chair" and "table" meant and made no mistakes all that evening. The next evening he was as accurate.

I often demonstrated his "tricks" to friends. One day I wished I hadn't. Our then small son said, "Jump on the table," when our dining-room table was set for dinner. The dog, having learned his lesson thoroughly, did just that!

Anyone with common sense and patience can train a dog to do any reasonable act. As in the case of man, he can never learn so many things that his brain becomes cluttered. The curious fact is that the more he learns, the easier he learns, just as you and I.

Always, when you are training, remember that he is a dog, not human. He has no imagination; he lives for the moment only. He cannot imitate or reason to any extent. He worships you for what you do for him and remains blindly loyal even to death. He can learn to react towards sounds, but he cannot put words together in his mind and come up with new thoughts. He has a prodigious memory. He can hear sounds you can't hear. He can smell odors that you can't even imagine. He feels pain through his skin less than you do, is less sensitive. He can stand long hours of exertion, and it does him good. He is a long way from being human, but he needs our protection. We made him what he is today, so different from his savage, wild ancestors. Let us remember these facts and treat him as a dog, our best animal friend, and he will repay every kindness a thousandfold.

Chapter Eight

BREEDING DOGS

In this section we shall consider some facts that are not known to everyone who decides to breed dogs. You may have raised a female puppy that you think, for some good reason, is worth reproducing. Perhaps you have decided that it will do the children good to learn about reproduction via the family pet. Or you may have embarked on commercial breeding to earn extra money or become devoted to dog breeding as a hobby.

Many facts that are commonplace to experienced dog breeders or to veterinarians are so new and novel to the inexperienced that a fairly full description of how to manage the problem of reproduction should be given.

THE BITCH IN HEAT

Every bitch can be expected to go through a mating cycle twice a year. The first cycle usually starts before the dog is a year old, but not until she is fully mature. One often hears inexperienced dog owners say, "Never breed a bitch at her first heat period; you wouldn't think it was right for a thirteen-year-old girl to have a baby, would you?" This is an absurd comparison. A thirteen-year-old girl has years to go to become a fully developed woman, but a bitch won't come in heat unless she is developed enough to bear a litter. She may not do quite as mature a job of raising her puppies as she would if older, but the difference is very slight. I've bred hundreds of bitches to studs at their first heats and always with excellent results. So have thousands of other owners.

The age at first heat—the age at maturity—depends on such factors as the rate of growth, the breed of dog, and the time of the year.

Bitches of small breeds start their first heat periods as young as six or seven months, while the bitches of giant breeds may be as late as fourteen or sixteen months.

The heat is also more or less dependent on the length of the day. The majority of bitches come in heat as the days grow longer and again when they grow shorter. Even moving bitches from the North to the deep South will completely upset the cycle. Bitches have been known to go out of heat in the North, be moved to the South and in two months be back in heat again, because of the much longer days.

How will you recognize when your bitch is coming into heat?

The first indication is an increased appetite. The second a noticeable uneasiness that she wants to go out and roam. Next her vulva will swell, and she may pass reddish fluid from it which you will mistake for blood. There is considerable blood in the discharge, but it is not all blood.

The male dogs of the neighborhood will be attracted and may seem to hold a camp meeting on your lawn. They may even break windows trying to get into the house. This problem can be avoided if your dog is small enough to be carried. Instead of letting her out to relieve herself carry her to your car, drive to a park or nearly vacant lot and let her eliminate there.

Heat lasts about twenty-two days from beginning to end, but the local dogs, once they have discovered an active bitch will continue to come around for more than thirty days. The way to end their visits is to let the bitch out where they can smell her. By the time she has ovulated, a hormone is manufactured that after a week is strong enough to produce a "keep away" odor. When the males smell this, they will stop calling.

HOW TO OBTAIN A STUD

The father of a litter of puppies supplies half their heredity. Books on genetics show you how, by an intricate process, the infinitely small genes and chromosomes of the male combine with those of the female to supply all the architectural plans for the new puppy.

What concerns us is heredity in the broader sense. We dog breeders can provide the example of how it pays to be careful in how we mate our dogs.

The first thing one should ask is: What is the purpose for which my dog's breed was developed? Is it a guard dog—a German police dog? Where can I sell the puppies? The Army and police will buy the big bold ones. There isn't much point in breeding the bitch to the gentlest possible stud because, unless the pups are for house dogs, temperament isn't so important. Perhaps the registered male down the street is good enough; we have seen how keen he is, and how he keeps intruders away. But does he have all the physical qualities that the show standard calls for? He should possess them without any glaring defect.

Perhaps your bitch is a beagle. Ask yourself: Am I interested in a house pet, or showing, or hunting? Beagle temperament is quite reliable because beagles are inexpensive as puppies, and those with evil temperaments may be destroyed;

there is no way to sell the nasty ones, and the police or Army won't take them.

If you want to breed show dogs, and your bitch is an excellent show type, you should disregard all of the local dogs because none is likely to be good enough. Long before your bitch comes into heat, you decide on a certain famous show champion, make arrangements for the service, and have her mated at the proper time. There are several reasons for such a decision. First, you will help improve the breed, and second, you will be able to sell your puppies for considerably more money than you could if you breed her to an unknown stud. Third, you can keep the best bitch to carry on with as well as a stud that may prove to be so good in shows that you can charge $25 to $50 stud fee for his services.

But let's suppose you are interested in producing puppies that can win in field trials. In that case you forget show-type appearance and select a famous stud whose pedigree is replete with field-trial champions. Again you will have helped improve your dogs and come out economically far better than if you had bred your bitch to any neighborhood beagle.

A single stud can be tremendously influential in breed improvement, and his record will be known by the quality of the dogs he sires; so you should find the best possible stud and pay the fee—the pups will be worth it. Many stud dog owners refuse to breed their dogs to any but outstanding bitches. You may feel that yours has every fine quality only to be disappointed at being refused a service. That means you are wasting your time breeding the bitch you own. Keep her for a pet and buy a better one for breeding. The owner of a fine stud is proud of the get of his dog. If your bitch is of poor quality, she will produce pups that will be a poor advertisement of the stud's quality as a sire.

The vast majority of dogs are simply pets. They should be

bred basically for good temperament. For a house pet, a cute mongrel is infinitely better to own than the finest show dog with an evil disposition.

WHEN TO BREED THE BITCH

If you decide you are going to breed your dog, you should understand enough about her reproductive system to know *when* to take her to a male stud. The mating cycle starts usually before the owner recognizes it. First, the ovaries, which are about as large as yellow eye beans, lose the so-called yellow bodies (corpora lutea) that prevent the heat period from beginning. When these have disappeared, eggs (ova) start developing, each in a sac that looks like a blister. When the sac is as large as a pea, it bursts from internal pressure. The eggs are released. The time this event (ovulation) occurs varies somewhat with the size of the bitch. Small breeds ovulate as early as the twelfth to fourteenth day of the heat, counting from the first swelling of the vulva, while large breeds ovulate from the fourteenth to the sixteenth day. The bitch should be bred accordingly. If she is bred earlier, the sperm from the male will die before they can fertilize the ova. The ideal time to mate is just after ovulation when the swelling of the vulva loses some of its congestion (called detumescence). Mating a day before or even two days before ovulation can produce full-size litters, but the one and two pup litters are often the result of mating as soon as the bitch will accept a male. One seldom hears of a small litter in a breed which normally produces five to twelve puppies when mating took place at or right after ovulation.

When a small bitch capable of having a normal litter has only one puppy, it usually is larger than it would have been had it been one of five or six. This means that the mother has a more difficult birth, and that smaller dogs may even need a Caesarean operation.

The length of time a bitch carries her puppies is sixty-one days from ovulation. All of the tables of the *gestation period*, as it is called, tell us sixty-three days but sixty-one is correct. The sixty-three is figured from the time of breeding, which is often as soon as the bitch is willing to accept the dog, and this is several days before ovulation.

DIAGNOSING PREGNANCY

If a bitch has ovulated, she will go through most of the phases of pregnancy whether she is bred or not. If she did not ovulate, you can expect her back in heat in about a month. If she did ovulate, even if the mating does not result in pregnancy, there will be a slight increase in her belly size and certainly some development of her udder (mammary glands). (This last is usually an excellent indication that the bitch is normal.) Sometimes when a bitch is mated too early or to an infertile male, she may develop pseudo-pregnancy and even produce milk. Don't be fooled by this condition and remember that it is a common, normal occurrence.

After twenty-four to twenty-eight days of pregnancy, you can clearly feel lumps in the bitch's abdomen which represent the developing fetuses surrounded by the placenta, fetal envelopes, some fluid, and the uterine wall. These lumps lie at fairly regular intervals much like the beans within the soft shell of a string bean, except that they are much larger. Their size is proportional to the size of the bitch.

At twenty-four days the lumps in a toy poodle are about three-eighths of an inch in diameter, at twenty-eight days, three-quarters of an inch. In an English setter or collie, the lumps are one-half inch at twenty-four days, as large as English walnuts at twenty-eight days. After thirty days, the lumps become so large and soft that only an expert can detect them, but by then the bitch's belly will have increased so much in size that her condition, unless she is pregnant with only one or two fetuses, is obvious.

WHELPING

By the fifty-ninth day the bitch's udder or breasts are well developed and the teats full of milk. A day or two before she is due she will become restless, looking for a bed. In a home she may go into a closet and scratch the shoes on the floor into a pile or if she finds a blanket, scratch it to try to form a bed. This is the time to prepare a bed for her.

If you observe a dog choosing and preparing a bed to whelp in, you'll find it is always saucer shaped. When the puppies are left alone, they roll into a group. If it is a hot day, they spread out. When the mother returns to the nest, she walks round and round often nosing them into a pile around which she lies. In this way she almost never crushes a puppy.

The worst kind of bed is a flat floor or concrete covered with rags. Puppies spread out instead of being in a group and so the dam often lies on one or more. The rags twist around the pups, or they crawl underneath. If the floor is concrete, they rub their navels against it, and the navels become worn away and infected so that a hole develops in the skin. Thousands of puppies are lost this way every year.

The ideal bed is a square one about six inches longer and wider than the bitch measures from the base of her tail to her nose. The sides should be from six inches to a foot high depending on the size of the bitch. The bed can be filled with some good bedding like straw, marsh hay, shredded dehydrated sugar cane, coarse shavings and formed into a saucer shape.

The bed should be placed in a quiet spot where there is as little coming and going as possible.

Of course, such a bed is not practical for a fancy poodle in an apartment because her long coat would scatter the bedding, so a flat bed with a piece of clean carpeting can be used, and the bitch should be watched so she does not smother a puppy when she lies down.

For a backyard whelping device, a wire bottom pen with hutch attached is hard to beat (see photo section). Thousands of puppies have been raised in them with excellent results. The bed in the hutch can be made of whatever appropriate material is available and should be saucer shaped.

The actual process of whelping usually gives the bitch or dam no pain and little inconvenience. She lies curled up or flat out. Her hormones cause the uterus to contract, much as peristalsis in the intestines causes food to move along. The last puppy in the Y-shaped uterus is forced into the birth canal. When the dam does some forcing by muscular contraction, the puppy is moved out. The mother at once licks it as dry as she can.

Sometimes the placenta comes away with the puppy, or its umbilical cord is connected to it. The bitch may sever the cord and pull until the placenta comes out. This she will consume herself. Usually the placenta is forced out ahead of the next puppy.

Sometimes two puppies are born so closely together that the dam only has time for one, and the fetal envelopes surround another pup so it cannot breathe. In these cases, the envelopes must be torn open to let the puppy breathe because the placenta is no longer connected to the mother's uterus, and there is no oxygen supply. This is a good reason for frequent inspection of the whelping bitch, especially of a valuable one.

If a puppy is partly out, and the bitch can't seem to expel it, help her by putting a cloth over it and pulling gently. Do this at an early stage or the puppy will die. If she shows she can't whelp take her to your veterinarian, and he can save her and some or all of her puppies by performing a timely Caesarean operation. Or he may be able to remove the first puppy with an instrument, afterwards the rest may be born normally. Or he may help deliver them all with an instrument.

SAVING PUPPIES

Sometimes a new puppy will be accidently removed from the nest, lose its mother, or be ignored by a dam that has developed a post partum fever and has no interest in her litter. These puppies, even those that appear dead, can often be saved. The first thing is to warm them. Don't depend on a stove or oven. Use hot water, almost as hot as your hand can stand. Then dip the puppies so deeply in the water that only their mouths and noses are above the surface. Be sure to keep the brain cases under, but don't let the noses or mouths submerge. If you are dealing with more than one puppy you can hold the heads between your fingers.

The heat exchange is very rapid so the water will cool quickly and must be heated with more hot water. After a considerable time you may see movement in a paw. Such a puppy can be saved. Gradually all with any life will respond. When they are wriggling and crying take them from the water, dry and put them in a warm place—back with the mother if possible.

Puppies whose mothers are unable to nurse them can be

saved by using modified cow's milk or special preparations and feeding with a bottle and nipple.

There is another way of feeding puppies, which I introduced back in 1930 when I was experimenting with artificial puppy milk. This is the tube method. You will find it described on page 160. It is very effective and the most efficient way I know of feeding pups too weak to nurse.

To start you can use a ten c.c. syringe and a catheter of some kind. (You can buy a female urethral catheter and syringe from some drug stores and from any surgical supply stores.) The open end needs to be cut down to fit the syringe. If you are uncertain as to whether the tube is in the gullet or the windpipe, put the pup on the table and hold the end to your ear and listen. If you have it in the windpipe, you can hear breathing.

I like a tube stiffer than a catheter and have found that after a while I can judge that it is in the stomach by the distance it goes. I use a polyethylene tube small enough so the end will fit over the syringe tube. It is better to insert the tube into the stomach and then connect the filled syringe. Press the plunger and transfer the warm milk to the puppy's stomach.

A twenty c.c. or even a fifty c.c. syringe is needed for puppies of large breeds.

By this method a litter can be fed in a few minutes. The tube and syringe should be kept scrupulously clean but need not be washed as it is transferred from pup to pup.

The tube method is quickest, but there are many other ways of feeding orphan puppies. I have made many styles of gang feeders or had glass blowers make them for me. After all the experimentation, I find that except for the tube method the easiest way of feeding even a litter is with a plastic bottle, and nipple, and a syringe needle. The warmed bottle is filled with milk at 100 degrees, the nipple put on, the needle pushed into the side of the bottle with the point sticking into the bottle's neck. This acts as an air valve. The pup sucks out the milk, and air runs through the needle into the bottle. You can see that the pup is getting milk by observing air bubbles going through the milk. As the puppies grow older and larger, the holes in the nipple can be enlarged slightly. In a few minutes each pup gets all he wants.

Keep the milk warm. A drop of less than 10 degrees will often discourage a young puppy from sucking. And tend to the toilet functions as soon as the pup is full.

How frequently must very young pups be fed? From a long series of tests, I have found that three feedings a day are insufficient, four are adequate, and five are ideal. By the time the pups are two weeks old their stomachs will stretch enough so that four feedings will suffice. When they are sixteen days old they can be taught to lap from a saucer.

You may have read that a medicine dropper can be used to feed puppies. Some books tell you that three or four dropperfuls are enough. This is true only for the very smallest breeds. A newborn beagle pup can take ten to fifteen c.c. (a medicine dropper holds about three-fourths of a c.c.). By the time a setter puppy is a week old, he will be taking four ounces or more at a feeding.

PUPPY SANITATION

Were it not for the way in which the mother animal of many related species tends to the sanitation of her litter of puppies, the beds or nests would soon be filthy. The mother wolf hollows out a saucer in a cave, and if that bed is observed, it is found to be free of feces and urine. Why? Because the mother licks her puppies clean; her system can absorb their wastes just as it did through the placenta before they were born.

Moreover, the puppies do not void automatically. They void only when the action is triggered by the lapping of the mother's tongue. This sensation causes a relaxation of the nerves that keep the sphincter muscles constricted. (Sphincter muscles are circular muscles around the anus and the urethra.)

This fact is surprisingly important to the puppy owner on two counts. The first is that in raising orphaned puppies, it is necessary to use a piece of absorbent cotton or soft paper and wipe it over the penis or vulva and anus. The sensation felt by the puppy will cause immediate voiding. If this is not done the puppy's bed will become dirty. The second is to show how closely voiding is linked to specific sensations. This knowledge is helpful in housebreaking. When the puppy grows older and holds more waste than the mother can manage, he is also old enough to void without the mother's having provided the stimulus. As was previously mentioned, puppies can then be conditioned to a new stimulus—the way the place where they void feels to their feet. Each time they void on a specific surface they are conditioned to use only that surface to void on. If they are reared on a wire bottom cage and you bring such a puppy into a home heated through a floor grating, you may be sure the puppy will void on the grating because it feels like his old cage.

Knowing these facts about natural animal sanitation should help you in training your puppy.

FOOD FOR YOUNG PUPPIES

There has been so much misinformation given out on this subject that you should learn the true facts about very early canine nutrition.

The first food for every dog is milk, but people unacquainted with the analysis of bitch's milk often believe that they should modify cow's milk by adding dextrose and reducing the fat to make the liquid resemble human milk. This is modifying in precisely the wrong way. What is needed is more fat, not less. Bitch's milk often contains 13 percent butterfat while human milk contains 3.5 percent and cow's milk 4 percent. Puppies can thrive on it for several weeks, provided they are not suffering from hookworms that cause anemia and lower the iron and salt content of the blood. Since milk is devoid of these minerals they should be added to the diet as early as possible, and puppies should be de-wormed by the time they are four weeks old. (See page 230.) The other lack in cow's milk is albumen. The protein in cow's milk is casein, while the protein in bitch's milk is nearly half albumen. Naturally, you may first think that you can increase the albumen by adding egg white, but egg white contains a substance called avidin that prevents digestion of the albumen. While cooking destroys avidin, it solidifies the egg white. Puppies manage to do all right without this substance, but do not grow quite so fast.

Raising the butterfat is easy because you can start with light cream, or if you have an homogenizer you can make high-fat milk by using one of the cooking oils. This, however, is a kennel proposition. Perhaps your best solution is to buy one of the powdered puppy milks, make a solution and feed that through a nipple.

If this food is not available, use cream. The following comparison among cow's milk, human milk, and bitch's milk will show you how close the cream is to bitch's milk.

COMPOSITION OF MILK

	FAT	PROTEIN	CARBOHYDRATE	ASH	WATER
Human	3.5	1.3	7.5	0.2	88
Cow	4.0	3.8	4.9	0.7	86.2
Goat	3.5	3.1	4.6	0.8	88.3
Bitch	11.2	5.7	3.1	1.3	78.7

Somehow the idea became prevalent that goat's milk is an excellent substitute for bitch's milk. The table above shows how wrong that idea is.

So much for the earliest puppy food—milk. The first solid food of the wild dog and many domestic puppies is predigested by the mother. When the puppies are about three weeks old, the mother goes afield, finds food, partially digests it with her highly acid stomach juice, returns home and regurgitates the food before the puppies. They pile into it and eat it ravenously. What's left is eaten by the mother, who then laps the puppies clean.

This food, too, is rich in fat and protein. Understanding the content will help you understand what is best to feed to newly weaned puppies. So many authors who do not comprehend these facts advise making the first solid food similar to that fed to human infants; again they are wrong, because the food should be high in fat and protein and contain enough hydrochloric acid to make it smell somewhat sour.

Puppies at fourteen to sixteen days can be taught to eat gruel. Smear some butter on the bottom of a saucer and let them lick it off. To wean them add one-eighth inch of puppy gruel. You can then feed them prepared puppy foods or make your own by mashing liver, bread, cream, and a little water together. Give the puppies some water if your gruel does not contain enough.

As they grow older feed the pups a well-tested puppy food four or five times a day. After a few weeks you can cut feedings to three times a day and by three months you need only feed them twice a day. Water should be available at all times.

PARASITES IN YOUNG PUPPIES

My son and I published a study showing the natural expectancy of parasites in dogs of all ages. The newer de-worming drugs will surely reduce these figures, but in 1967, 50 percent of all baby puppies had roundworms and 20 percent had hookworms.

No puppy can thrive with many parasites poisoning it or sucking blood as hookworms do. Therefore, by the time the pup is three weeks old, either have a fecal examination made by your veterinarian or give the puppy piperazine according to directions. This will destroy the roundworms. A new drug, Task, will destroy both roundworms and hookworms. These are the two internal parasites that you need worry about when your puppy is an infant.

Externally, puppies may contract lice from their mothers and fleas from their environment. As they wander afield ticks may attach themselves to their skin. Even in the nest one species of tick can live part of its life cycle on a puppy and often does.

You must keep these external parasites in check if you want your dog to grow up healthy. Fleas and lice multiply with incredible rapidity. I always hang a Vapona bar above the beds in my puppy pens. The fumes destroy all fleas and lice. You would be wise to do the same.

BABY PUPPY AILMENTS

Many people believe puppies receive certain immunities from their mothers, which carry through their infancy. But there are diseases and ailments quite common in pups, notably diarrhea. When young dogs become overheated, or if the dam does not clean them, an entire litter may die. Quite often the diagnosis is "acid milk," which is nonsense because the bitch's milk should be acid. Early treatment with anti-diarrheal drugs by your veterinarian can usually save the litter.

Coccidiosis is another serious ailment that is not found in well-cared-for baby puppies, but is very common in older pups, as we have seen.

Worn navels, as previously mentioned, have to be watched for, unless the bed is soft and the puppies' bellies can't touch concrete or rough boards.

Sometimes puppies can't seem to suck properly because of cleft palates. Open the mouth and observe whether this is the trouble. Hare lips are common, too. It is usually better to destroy such puppies. Operations are not always successful and are expensive.

If your puppy sleeps on shavings be careful that one never gets caught in its upper throat. It must be removed, or the little thing will starve.

Hip weakness

There are several causes for hip weakness; one is called hip-dysplasia. Dog owners are hearing a great deal about it, but since it does not appear until the later months of puppy growth, it is not detected at the age when most puppies change hands. X-rays taken by a definite plan may show that the hip socket into which the ball on the end of the thigh bone (femur) fits, is too shallow to be normal.

The cause is not known for certain. Heredity is suspected and so is nutrition. Some attribute the trouble to a lack of exercise. It is seen most frequently in the big breeds and in dogs overfed with dietary supplements such as vitamins and minerals.

If your puppy, when grown, has a normal gait, can jump

up quickly and agilely and can hurdle fences, hip-dysplasia need not be of any concern.

UNWANTED PUPPIES

Suppose your bitch mates with a dog in the neighborhood, when the last thing you want is a litter of mongrel puppies. What should you do?

Until recently, it was necessary to let her go through pregnancy and destroy the puppies at birth. But now a drug called Malucidin has been discovered, which your veterinarian can inject into your bitch's vein, that causes the puppies and placenta to disappear. It in no way prevents future pregnancies or harms the bitch in any way. I have produced resorption in over two hundred bitches. One was resorbed seven times and then permitted to carry a litter, and she whelped nine healthy puppies. If you have delayed having the bitch's pups resorbed until the last one-third of pregnancy, she will abort, passing the puppies and the placentas which you will have to clean up. The mother who was not ready to deliver will simply ignore the litter.

As this is written, the Food and Drug Administration has not yet passed on the drug, so your veterinarian will have to use it on an experimental basis, which hundreds have been doing.

SELLING PUPPIES

Advertising is the best way to sell puppies.

First, consider carefully who will want to buy the breed you have to sell, and use the proper medium to sell your product. There's little use in advertising in a breeder's magazine because breeders themselves have pups to sell; they aren't looking to buy. For housedog pets like poodles, spaniels, Chihuahuas, the newspaper pet column is usually productive. For persons wanting watchdogs, city newspapers are also good. Hunting dogs sell best in magazines read by hunters; farm dogs sell in farming magazines.

One of the strange facts about newspaper advertising is that puppies sell better in nearby cities than they do in your own. So advertise in them, as well as in your local paper.

If you have expensive puppies, put the price in your ad. If you simply say, poodles, etc., and give your address or phone number, be assured that dozens of persons wanting $5 dogs will plague you.

Make the advertisement as attractive to the buyer as you possibly can. If the puppies are partially housebroken, say so. If they have been permanently protected against distemper, hepatitis, leptospirosis, say so. The word "vaccinated," which so many ads include, is almost meaningless. If the puppies are from field-trial champions, say so, or if they are from the great show dog Champion Cheesecake, include that in your ad. If a certain color is most stylish, and if your puppies are of that color, the descriptive word will pull inquiries. It often pays to name all the colors of the puppies in a litter, especially of poodles.

Your ad should be as specific as possible to avoid needless calls and unproductive replies.

If you have a partly grown litter or just one puppy, the easiest way to unload it is to first spend some time in training. Teach the pup to jump in a chair, run to a corner and sit, shake hands, lie down. These simple responses can be very quickly taught. Show them to the prospective buyer and the puppy is not only irresistible, but also worth more money. If you spend fifteen minutes every other day, in ten days your pup responds to five different signals. Then you can include in your advertisement the words, "trained for some tricks." That will surely step up inquiries.

One *don't*. Don't price the puppies too high or too low. If they are too high in price (exception—trained pups), you will sell them very slowly, if at all. If you price them too low, buyers will expect them to grow into inferior specimens.

When prospective customers arrive to see the puppies, show the mother and what a fine, gentle dog she is. Father, too, if you own him. Needless to say, all the litter and the parents must look desirable and *clean*. If the breed is one that needs clipping, have them all clipped to look as cute and attractive as possible. If the parents are trained, show them off. A wise buyer, as we said earlier, wants to know about the parents.

Remember that Rin Tin Tin and Lassie are what made prospective buyers want a dog of those breeds. They don't realize all the work that went into having those dogs respond as they do. If your parent dog or dogs can perform well, they will prove great assets to you in selling your puppies.

Index

636.7
W

Whitney, Leon F.

How to select,
train, and
breed your dog

DATE		